Pocket Underground map of about 1908 showing the Charing Cross, Euston & Hampstead Railway in relation to the other electrified Underground lines at that time. Although the various lines were then in different ownership, it had already been agreed to promote them as a single network by the name UNDERGROUND.

Colour illustration from a 1920s' trade magazine or catalogue giving an impression of the rebuilt Tottenham Court Road station at intermediate level.

The Last Link

The First 30 Years of The Hampstead Tube

1907–1937

by

Mike Horne FCILT, MIRO

Published jointly by London Underground Ltd (Northern Line) and Nebulous Books

in commemoration of the 100TH anniversary of

THE CHARING CROSS, EUSTON & HAMPSTEAD RAILWAY

www.tfl.gov.uk
www.nebulousbooks.com
www.metadyne.co.uk

© 2007 Mike Horne
ISBN 978 0 9507416 6 6

Cover design by Elaine Chambers
Book design and production by Douglas Rose
Printed by Moorprint Services Ltd, London

Acknowledgements
Tickets are reproduced from three private collections and carry these numbers:
Godfrey R. Croughton: 1, 2, 5, 6, 7, 8, 15, 16, 17, 18, 20, 21, 22, 24, 25,
    and the paper ticket on the inside front cover;
Jim Connor: 4, 3, 10, 19 and the three on the outside back cover;
Mike Horne: 9, 12, 11, 13, 14, 23, 26, 27.

All cover images (except tickets) are copyright TfL and reproduced courtesy of
London Transport Museum:
Hampstead Railway Non-Stop (poster, 1910),
London's Playground Hampstead Heath (poster, 1908),
The Soonest Reached at Any Time – Golders Green (poster, 1908),
Hampstead Line – Golders Green (poster, 1912),
London's Latest Suburbs (book cover, 1910).

All other illustrations are copyright TfL
and reproduced courtesy of London Transport Museum, with the exception of:
Mike Horne collection: front colour section map, Tottenham Court Road (p ii),
Prospectus (p5), *The Mole* (p9), Golders Green platform (ex postcard, original
source unknown) (p10), Euston plan (p23), timetable cover (p41), both
photographs (p43), signal diagrams (pp45–51, 52 and 53), photograph (p50),
photograph (p52), diagram (p54), Rule Book (p55), exam papers (p58),
photograph (p61), *Hints to Passengers* leaflet (inside back cover).

The Railway Engineer: drawing (p12)
Railway Magazine: drawing (p33), photograph (p46),
photograph (p60), photograph (p64).

Doug Rose: tile pattern realization (p25).

Further Reading
Additional historical context may be gained from:
Desmond F. Croome and Alan A. Jackson, *Rails Through the Clay*. Harrow Weald:
Capital Transport, 1993 (2nd edition). A detailed study of all of London's tube
railways.

Douglas Rose, *The London Underground: A Diagrammatic History*. North Finchley,
Douglas Rose, 2007 (8th edition). This is a poster-sized diagram, reminiscent of
the London Underground 'map', and shows opening and closing dates for all
stations and lines across the entire network, as well as all station name changes.

Douglas Rose, *Tiles of the Unexpected, Underground*. North Finchley, Douglas Rose,
2007. This is a copiously illustrated large-format book and includes realizations of
all the platform tile patterns on the Yerkes network; with detailed station plans.

Foreword

Although most London Underground lines have been built in stages, the Northern line is perhaps unusual in that it has been stitched together from no less than three separate lines, plus a number of extensions.

One of these lines is the Charing Cross, Euston & Hampstead, known as 'the Hampstead tube'. As Mike Horne ably illustrates, this railway was built at a time of great change. It is fitting that its centenary also occurs at a time of major refurbishment, with new rolling stock in the late 90s, and station and signalling upgrades in the present decade.

Contemporary accounts of the opening in 1907 recognized the great scale of its construction, and its importance to Government of the day. David Lloyd George MP, then President of the Board of Trade, drove the first train from Charing Cross. Later, at a celebratory lunch in the depot buildings at Golders Green, he noted: "That it was a wonder, when thinking of what the underground railways did for the traffic of London, how London got on without them years ago".

The purpose of this book is to celebrate and learn from the Hampstead tube's construction and early life. It is now an integral part of the Northern line, which conveys 0.75 million customers daily. It is to them, and the 2000 staff who operate and maintain it, that this book is dedicated.

David Millard (General Manager, Northern Line)
30th March 2007

CONTENTS

EXPLANATION OF STANDARD SIGNAL DIAGRAM SYMBOLS

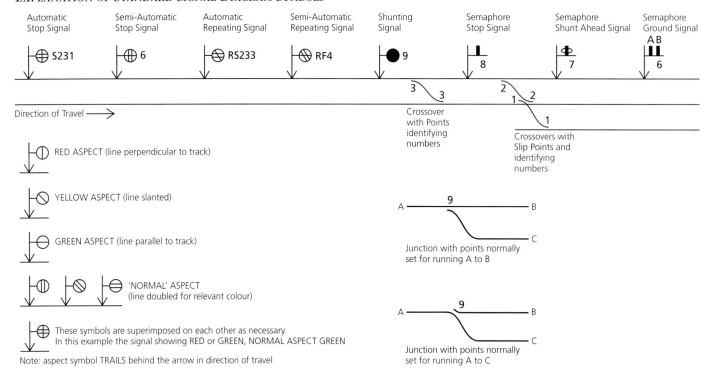

Automatic Stop Signal	Semi-Automatic Stop Signal	Automatic Repeating Signal	Semi-Automatic Repeating Signal	Shunting Signal	Semaphore Stop Signal	Semaphore Shunt Ahead Signal	Semaphore Ground Signal
S231	6	RS233	RF4	9	8	7	6

Direction of Travel ⟶

RED ASPECT (line perpendicular to track)

YELLOW ASPECT (line slanted)

GREEN ASPECT (line parallel to track)

'NORMAL' ASPECT (line doubled for relevant colour)

These symbols are superimposed on each other as necessary. In this example the signal showing RED or GREEN, NORMAL ASPECT GREEN

Note: aspect symbol TRAILS behind the arrow in direction of travel

Crossover with Points identifying numbers

Crossovers with Slip Points and identifying numbers

Junction with points normally set for running A to B

Junction with points normally set for running A to C

NOTES AND ABBREVIATIONS

This book deploys imperial units of measurement that relate more appropriately to the period of history it covers. Rather than disrupt the flow of text by inserting modern units as well, a table of equivalents is given below.

Unit	Abbreviation	Metric Equivalent
mile	M	1.6093km
yard	yd	0.9144m
foot	ft	0.3048m
inch	in	25.4mm
shilling	s	5p (or one twentieth of a pound)
penny	d	one twelfth of a shilling
horse power	hp	unit of power equivalent to 745.7 watts

Other Abbreviations		Explanation
alternating current	ac	
direct current	dc	
kilowatt	kW	equivalent to 1000 watts
volt	V	the unit of electrical pressure

INTRODUCTION

This book is really a celebration of two events. First, it celebrates the centenary of a huge part of London's Northern Line, the Charing Cross, Euston & Hampstead Railway, which opened on 22nd June 1907 and now forms the vital core of the Charing Cross, Highgate and Edgware branches. Secondly, it celebrates the completion of London's largest orgy of tube railway construction: three new railways serving 42 entirely new stations (with five more supplementing existing stations). This incredible aspiration was brought to life by the energy of a colourful American visionary and his brilliant team of compatriots, and his success forever changed the transport habits of Londoners. Such astonishing enterprise satisfied central London's need for rapid transit for decades—there were no new railways across the capital for another sixty years when the Victoria Line was built—and is surely a cause of celebration. The Charing Cross, Euston & Hampstead Railway was the last of the three lines to open and with nothing further in prospect was termed 'The Last Link'.

There are already many words written about the Northern Line, and more specifically about the Hampstead Railway—a catchier title than the Charing Cross, Euston & Hampstead Railway, and a contraction that caught on immediately. In consequence this book will focus on more detailed highlights of its evolution before the Second World War, to give more of a flavour of its operations. It is hoped that this will also impart some new and interesting material, while still covering the basic ground.

PART ONE
A BRIEF HISTORY OF THE
CHARING CROSS, EUSTON & HAMPSTEAD RAILWAY
UNTIL THE MID 1930s

EARLY TUBE RAILWAYS IN LONDON

A tube railway is one driven through the ground from occasional deep shafts, and is characterized by its separate circular iron tunnels for each direction of traffic. Before tube railways existed London's earliest underground lines were built just under the surface and were really small-scale main line railways within covered trenches whose construction was enormously disruptive— so unappealingly disruptive that it was unfeasible to bring them into the heart of central London. Tube railway construction solved the problem as inconvenience was substantially confined to the sites around the working shafts and tunnelling could proceed more or less invisibly. The first 'tube', as they became known informally, was the Tower Subway, opened in 1870; this quarter-mile single tunnel tube ran under the Thames near the Tower of London and proved to its promoter (the bridge engineer Peter William Barlow) that it was possible to use the same form of construction for building horizontal tunnels as were used for sinking iron caissons for bridges. The breakthrough was the use of a tunnelling shield (invented by Sir Marc Isambard Brunel, father of Isambard Kingdom Brunel with whom he collaborated on building the brick tunnel under the Thames at Rotherhithe). Barlow produced a cylindrical iron 'shield', forced into the tunnel face by screw jacks, which allowed the miners to excavate the spoil safely from within. When sufficient ground ahead had been dug away the shield was jacked forward again and a ring of segmented, flanged cast iron pieces quickly erected behind, the whole lot being firmly bolted together. By repeating this process an iron tunnel resulted, made firm and watertight by injecting cement grout into any remaining void between the tunnel rim and the surrounding ground. The Tower Subway was tiny, with tunnels a clear internal diameter of just 6ft 7³/4ins, within which a 2¹/2 feet gauge track was laid allowing a tiny, single, cable-hauled car to be dragged in either direction as required—the train service only lasted a few months but the subway remained open as a foot tunnel until the opening of Tower Bridge in 1896 rendered it unnecessary (though it remains in use as a service tunnel for utilities).

Though an engineering success, it was not until 1890 that the first 'proper' tube railway opened—the City & South London Railway (CS&LR)—running between the City and Stockwell. This was a standard gauge electric railway (the first in London), though built in tunnels some of which were just 10ft 2ins internal diameter, resulting in rather cramped carriage space. The diminutive trains were locomotive-hauled; the deep platforms were reached by hydraulic lifts and while the running tunnels were built of circular iron the station tunnels were brick-built with a flattened base, more like main line railway tunnels in shape. The construction methods were broadly successful and used new techniques like hydraulically-driven tunnelling shields and some construction in compressed air to keep water out of the works while tunnelling was in progress. The railway gave a tremendous boost to the technology of tube railway construction and operation; unfortunately, this particular little line was financially dubious despite significant later extensions towards Clapham and Euston. Commercial success was dogged partly by the enterprise's limited capacity, partly because its pioneer technology needed early replacement and partly because it ran under roads well served with other forms of transport, lessons its successor's would need to learn.

THE ORIGIN OF THE
CHARING CROSS, EUSTON & HAMPSTEAD RAILWAY

It was the City & South London's technical success that seeded many new schemes for tube railways across the capital. One of the quickest off the mark was the Hampstead, St Pancras & Charing Cross Railway, a parliamentary bill for which (among several others) was presented to the 1892 parliamentary session—at that time all railway works needed a private Act of Parliament. This line was to run from a point at the junction of Strand and Southampton Street via Charing Cross Road, Tottenham Court Road, Hampstead Road, Camden High Road, Chalk Farm Road, Haverstock Hill to Hampstead High Street. A branch line was to diverge from the main line immediately north of the Euston Road

to run eastwards under Drummond Street and the Midland Railway's great train shed at St Pancras, to terminate under the forecourt of the Great Northern Railway's King Cross station where it met York Road. The tube station was to be linked to St Pancras station by a bridge across Pancras Road, joining the balcony next to the station's eastern access steps. An intermediate station was planned along the branch at Euston, close to the London & North Western Railway station. The bill received the royal assent on 24th August 1893, though during the parliamentary process the name had changed to the Charing Cross, Euston & Hampstead Railway (CCE&HR) following Midland Railway opposition to the section between Chalton Street and King's Cross which had to be abandoned, leaving just Euston on the branch.

Fewer stations were originally intended than were subsequently built. Charing Cross station was to have been north of the Strand on the eastern corner of Agar Street, with a long subway under the Strand to the South Eastern Railway (SER) station. The station platforms at Charing Cross were to lie beneath the Strand, aiming due east, towards the City, and needed to be approached by a ferociously sharp curve from the Charing Cross Road. The Oxford Street station site was on the north west corner of the Tottenham Court Road intersection, opposite the Central London Railway station. The next station, Euston Road, seems to have been intended in Hampstead Road, just south of Eden Street, though an alternative site was available south of Euston Road fronting Tottenham Court Road. Two sites were also available for both Mornington Crescent and Chalk Farm, in each case including the sites where the stations are now. Hampstead and Belsize Park are at current locations though a second small site was available at Hampstead. At Euston the station was intended on the north side of Drummond Street in the block bounded by Cardington Street and Whittlebury Street. A further station at the junction of Hampstead and Kentish Town Roads was considered but not initially pursued, probably since it was not far away from Mornington Crescent.

Although the (C&SLR) tunnels were considered too small the 1893 act confined the Hampstead Railway to twin iron tunnels not exceeding 11ft 6ins diameter (except on curves and at crossovers) and station tunnels not exceeding 25 feet. It is observed the deposited plans quote standard tunnel diameter to be 11ft 5ins. Access to the platforms was to be via stairs and hydraulic or other lifts, and trains were to be operated by cable traction, electricity or other approved means (not being steam traction). There was at that time concern that electric traction would not have been adequate to deal with the 1 in 24 gradient necessary between Chalk Farm and Hampstead, but by the following year electric traction had been decided upon.

The Railway was promoted by seven businessmen including Joseph Browne-Martin (a director of the Westminster Electric Supply Corporation) and Edwin Levy; these two were to become directors of J. Lyons & Co Ltd (the caterers) the following year when it became a public company. Others included Viscount Grimston, Sir Frederick Johnstone, baronet (who lived in Dumfries), and a Henry Montague Smith, who may have had connections with the Westminster Free Library. By the following year Joseph Lyons himself had been roped into the venture, as if he hadn't enough to occupy him with his relaunched company, together with the Marquess of Ailesbury, one Henry Augustus Brudenell Bruce, who was also Chairman of Meux & Co, the Brewers. Edwin Levy died in 1895.

The promoters thought they had chosen a good route, with significant profit potential. In December 1893 Douglas and Francis Fox, and James Greathead, were appointed engineers, conditional on the shares being allotted, but therein lay a problem. The prospectus issued in 1894 suggested the line could be built and equipped for £1,888,000 (about £1bn–£1.5bn today in terms of comparable works) and set out to offer 141,600 £10 shares, the balance of £472,000 being raised by debentures guaranteeing a 4 per cent return. It was suggested that if an average of only 75 passengers entered each train anywhere during each trip, and paid an average fare of just 1³/4d, then this would generate income of £155,000 a year; with estimated working expenses of just £49,500, and interest of £18,880, a profit would be left of £68,380, enough to reward shareholders with a handsome 6 per cent. How wrong this proved.

Despite the promises of generous riches, investors were slow to come forward and the directors had to content themselves with keeping the scheme alive, for the compulsory purchase powers lasted only three years. The expensive business of maintaining the parliamentary powers and developing and improving on the route resulted in further powers being sought in 1897, 1898, 1899 and 1900, by the end of which little capital had been promised. However, the route had been improved. The 1898 Act altered the southern end of the line south of the Garrick Theatre so it terminated under the rear of No 23 Craven Street (parallel to the western edge of Charing Cross main line station), stopping immediately short of the Avenue Theatre and aiming towards the river rather than the City; the site for the station building is not clear, but may have been at the north end of Craven Street a few yards from the SE&CR station. The new route included two severe 4-chain reverse curves and one 6-chain curve in order to avoid St Martins-in-the-Fields parish church which sat upon the direct route.

A further attempt to raise capital was made in 1898. By this time the railway was apparently under the influence of what was shortly to become the South Eastern & Chatham Railway (SE&CR), a managing committee of the South Eastern and the London, Chatham & Dover Railways. Three of the five directors were directors of the emerging committee; one of these gentlemen was Sir David Salomons, son of the famous banker and himself a notable polymath, an engineer, inventor and in 1895 convener of Britain's first motor show in Tunbridge Wells (this may also have been a World's first) and he is reputed to have been Britain's second motor car owner. Salomons wrote a standard work on electric lighting and management of accumulators that went through many editions and we may safely presume he understood the issues around electricity generation. Browne-Martin (also still in the electricity supply business) and Grimston were still involved, the latter meanwhile having succeeded to the Earldom of Verulam, but the others had by now gone. The Hampstead Railway appears to have had some strategic importance to the SE&CR and considerable through traffic was dreamed of. Estimated traffic levels had increased to generate prospective income of £182,291 and the amount left for dividends had dropped to 4 per cent, reflecting revised market expectations. This did not generate the enthusiasm necessary to allot the shares and the railway carried on updating its powers in the absence of any immediate probability of starting work. The prospectus also mentions plans to build a second branch, to Kentish Town Midland Railway station and that a $2^{1}/_{2}$-minute core service was to operate, implying a $7^{1}/_{2}$-minute interval on each branch.

The 1899 Act was drawn more widely than the prospectus. One new feature was to extend the Euston branch northwards along Seymour and Eversholt Streets (putting Euston on the main line, the direct line along the Hampstead Road being abandoned). The Euston station site was also moved across the road to the south eastern corner of Melton Street and Drummond Street, partly on the site of the Henry Moore dining rooms; this was almost certainly because Euston main line station was in the process of expanding westwards along Drummond Street, completely obliterating Whittlebury Street and the initial tube station site. The new route brought the railway towards Mornington Crescent beneath Eversholt Street rather than the Hampstead Road; the 1898 prospectus still refers to a station here and the site in the apex of the road junction was the better one. A new station was authorized at Camden Town with the building in the Apex of Camden High Street and Kentish Town Road (perhaps rendering nearby Mornington Crescent unnecessary). A new station site was also authorized in Charing Cross Road, on the corner of Cranbourn Street.

The Act authorized the Camden Town–Kentish Town branch with the terminus next to the Midland Railway station; the line was to have continued a little way beyond, along Highgate Road, to reach an improved depot and power station site in the block of land north of Lady Somerset Road (part of this site had already been put to use by the Midland Railway for a power station of its own). The Kentish Town depot was to have been reached by a single track tunnel rising at an alarming $1:9^{1}/_{2}$ gradient, and one quite impractical for electric traction suggesting rope haulage might have been contemplated. It appears a depot had originally been proposed at Chalk Farm, where the line was quite shallow,

and the limits of deviation suggest a possible site on the east side of Chalk Farm Road south of Belmont Street. As the 1898 prospectus indicates, the decision to build a branch to Kentish Town seems to have been encouraged by warmer relations with the Midland Railway and the 1899 Act endorses an agreement of 22nd June 1899 between the Hampstead Railway and both the SE&CR and Midland Railway for the development of through traffic between Charing Cross (SE&CR) and Kentish Town (Midland) to, from and via the Hampstead Railway. Through traffic was to be encouraged and if tickets to SE&CR and Midland destinations were sold from Hampstead stations the latter made a 15 per cent commission. Perhaps following experience on the Central London Railway (a tube opened in 1900) the Act increased the maximum permitted tunnel size from 11ft 6ins to 13ft.

THE AMERICANS TO THE RESCUE

Finding itself unable to raise cash in Britain representatives of the Hampstead Railway sought support in New York and were eventually put in contact with the influential traction financier Charles Yerkes, whom they met in July 1899. The great man was offered the company and its parliamentary rights for just $200,000 (£41,000) providing he took over the construction contracts with Price & Reeves (signed in 1897); this contractor now numbered amongst the current promoters and therefore had a considerable interest in the line being built. Buying the contracts would effectively commit Yerkes to building the line. It was not until August 1900 that he agreed to finance its construction which he thought would cost some $13m (£2.7m), which was double the first estimate; he thought it would take just two years to complete. Although he was long familiar at first hand with London's traffic difficulties his decision to build the Hampstead Railway was influenced by a personal inspection of the route where he was amazed at the backward nature of the transport facilities provided, together with its profit-making potential. In the end he paid over to the railway £100,000, including enough to cover the parliamentary deposit which was locked up until the line opened.

Having got the bit between his teeth with the Hampstead scheme he became involved with plans to electrify the

Metropolitan District Railway (today's District Line) and that led to schemes to build other dormant or bankrupt tube schemes out of which emerged today's Piccadilly and Bakerloo Lines. When the full magnitude of Yerkes's enterprises became clear he was obliged to revise his financing plans by establishing a holding company (the grandly titled Underground Electric Railways Company of London Ltd, or UERL for short) charged with raising about £16m in all; only £5m was to come from the issue of shares, the rest from a raft of banking instruments which brought money pouring in from New York, Boston, Amsterdam, Frankfurt and Paris (amongst other places)—there was also some British input, mainly from Speyer Brothers who had orchestrated some of this activity.

Prior to work commencing on any of Yerkes's new tube railways the UERL determined that it would itself undertake total responsibility for their construction, including building the Hampstead Railway. The UERL would negotiate new construction contracts using existing main contractors (where appointed) but seeking the economies of scale that such an approach would offer. The £2.4m UERL contract with the Hampstead Railway was agreed on 3rd July 1902, back to back with a subcontract with Price & Reeves to construct the stations, platforms and tunnels (the UERL subsequently let other contracts for equipping the line). The initial specification was for a quality of railway 'no less than that of the Central London', from Charing Cross to Hampstead and Kentish Town, built in tunnels of 11ft 6ins diameter, with crossovers at each terminus. Intermediate stations were still planned as previously described and these plans confirm that the new station at 'Mother Red Cap' (Camden Town) had superseded the plan for one at Mornington Crescent. The Underground's contract called for each station to have a single 18ft stair shaft with a double spiral of stairs (one for each direction of traffic) and a single shaft for the lifts, either of 23ft diameter (for two lifts) or 30ft (for three lifts); on the other hand the Price & Reeves contract, signed the same day, called for the stair shaft and two 23ft lift shafts, which is largely what was built. Lighting was to be by electricity with gas as a standby for emergencies or if the power plant was shut down at night; illumination was to be assisted by finishings in glazed white tiling like the Central London Railway.

Cover from the Hampstead's unsuccessful first share prospectus.

Platforms were to be in 21ft internal diameter tunnels (within finishings), 250ft long and made of wood 11ft wide comprising 4-inch planking. This was intended to provide accommodation for 5-coach trains (maximum) seating 240 passengers. Rolling stock was to comprise 100 cars (75 trailers and 25 motor cars) 'equal in quality' to those employed on the New York Elevated Railway from 1892. A train service interval of five minutes was planned for, supervised by a 'complete system' of signals with suitable cabins. A suitable depot and generating station was also required to be furnished.

The Americans soon concluded that the Hampstead Railway was a little constrained by the inherited plans and that modest extension was called for. They sought and obtained on 18th November 1902 a further Act of Parliament for extending the Kentish Town branch via Tufnell Park to a new terminus at Highgate (Archway), which was then a commercial centre and busy road intersection; it had been hoped to get powers to go on further, to Bishops Road, just beyond the Great Northern Railway (GNR) station at Highgate, but this was disallowed. The Hampstead branch was likewise projected almost 1 1/2 miles north west to emerge in the open air immediately north of the Hampstead ridge at a remote crossroads near the hamlet of Golders Green. By repute, Yerkes had it in mind to profit from increases in land value which he judged would result from the building of a railway. Whether that was true or not, he thought quite correctly that people would follow anyhow and they would become regular fare payers; just as relevantly it provided a far more spacious location for a depot and power station. The extension also required Hampstead station to be built somewhat deeper than planned, which would ease gradients to the south, and the Act provided for another station in Tottenham Court Road, between Goodge Street and Tottenham Street (today's Goodge Street, already anticipated in the construction contracts). In addition it had proved difficult to pursue the Oxford Street station site on the corner of Tottenham Court Road and powers were obtained for an underground ticket hall beneath the road junction itself.

At the south end, further agonizing about the terminal arrangements resulted in the line being re-routed nearer the Duncannon Street/Adelaide Street intersection, crossing Strand opposite the SE&CR station, and then taking the line of Villiers Street towards Yerkes's District Railway station at Charing Cross where an interchange would be possible. Connection with the SE&CR would be retained by means of a new station north of Strand, on the east side of Adelaide Street, with subway link between the two railways.

Once Euston had been placed on the main line, the vicious curves taking the line between Hampstead Road and Drummond Street were now considered unnecessarily sharp and the 1902 Act eased them by starting them further south, requiring Euston Road station to be resited south of that road instead of in Hampstead Road; the new station did not (as first planned) front Tottenham Court Road but occupied a whole block of buildings fronting Warren Street (numbers 74–77) and Euston Road (odd numbers 289–295); while number 77 was being pulled down number 78 subsided and had to be entirely rebuilt at the Underground's expense—ironically the Underground later purchased No 78 for demolition when the station was rebuilt in 1932-3. Even while construction was pressed ahead additional changes were planned which resulted in a further Act on 11 August 1903 which authorized additional stations at North End (south of Golders Green), Castle Road (south of Kentish Town) and Mornington Crescent, the latter really being a reinstatement of the earlier plan on virtually the same site; the act also adjusted the route between Hampstead and Golders Green.

The new works required a supplemental agreement (signed on 14th June 1904) whereby the UERL agreed to build the extra stations and other bits of railway latterly sanctioned by Parliament, even though construction was already under way. The agreement also ratified abandonment of the depot at Kentish Town, rearranged station at Charing Cross and the taking of power from a central generating station at Lots Road rather than the Hampstead Railway having its own at Golders Green. There were many subsequent departures from both of these agreements with decisions apparently taken 'on the fly' without wasting time settling the legal niceties first. But matters did need regularizing, and desultory discussion rumbled on until an agreement of 25th

July 1910 put everything to bed. The UERL was remunerated for their 'extra' efforts largely with Hampstead stock and rights to surplus land rather than extracting precious and diminishing cash. The agreement also required the Hampstead Railway to accept things that had evidently not been expected, such as a joint station with the Piccadilly at Leicester Square.

While the contractual arrangements were sorted out, work needed putting in hand and started in July 1902 when some houses at the foot of Haverstock Hill were demolished at the Chalk Farm station site. By April 1903 activity was in hand at further sites for Belsize Park, Camden Town, Euston and Leicester Square (joint with the Piccadilly). Tunnel construction began in September 1903, with (incredibly) tunnelling three quarters complete by the following October, and while the rest was substantially ready by April 1906 it was not finished until December 1906 owing to local complications. The tunnelling on the Hampstead was undertaken mainly by hand mining using the well established 'Greathead Shields'; these were improved versions of the older Barlow shields and involved hydraulically pushing a protective steel drum into the clay ahead of the miners while they cut away the clay face. About a quarter of the line used mechanical excavation using the 'Price' rotary excavator where a rotating drum was mounted at the cutting face within the shield, the drum being fitted with teeth that carved the clay away from the face and greatly speeded construction (although a maximum rate of 160 feet per week was quoted it was difficult to keep an accurate alignment with the excavator requiring tedious adjustment of the segments later, and it was some years before it was really perfected). As already stated, the internal tunnel diameter had been intended to be 11ft 6ins and although authority had been granted to increase this substantially, the UERL finally opted simply to reduce the flange size, winning another 2^{1}/$_{4}$ inches and producing the odd size of 11ft 8^{1}/$_{4}$ins. This was cost effective at the time but perhaps today's users might have preferred the larger trains that would have been possible in 13ft tunnels.

At Charing Cross the UERL had found itself in some difficulty. Although a site north of Strand was planned it really wanted a better link with the SE&CR and received further powers in 1903 to build under the eastern part of the SE&CR station forecourt; however the powers were restrictive and forbade interference with the surface, which made construction very difficult. The Hampstead Railway obtained yet more powers in 1905, largely to authorize improved arrangements for its Charing Cross station; these powers eased matters only slightly, permitting construction under the western part of the forecourt with temporary occupation of the surface as short as possible (the SE&CR unsurprisingly wanted minimal interference at this cramped site). Before matters were resolved a terrible accident occurred on 5th December 1905 when the arched roof of the SE&CR station collapsed (this was caused by the snapping of a critical tie-rod allowing the roof load to spread sideways taking the supporting walls away on the Craven Street side, and was nothing to do with the tube). Although only six people were killed, this devastating incident rendered the station unusable for three months. Although one might have thought the forecourt would have been required entirely for recovery and repair purposes the UERL got permission to open up part of it and get on with constructing its own station beneath, settling the site problem once and for all. In that time the ticket hall area was excavated down to 12 feet depth, one lift shaft was sunk to its full depth, steel beams were erected over the void and the forecourt surface made good. Far more difficulty followed as the booking hall needed excavating to its full depth, the retaining walls needing to be build downwards from initial construction which already bore a load, and the remaining shafts sunk, all with limited surface access. With all this going on it is no surprise the Hampstead's awkward further projection to the District's station at the other end of Villiers Street was postponed indefinitely, and the line stopped abruptly at the platform headwall at the south end of the station.

The 1905 Act received the Royal Assent on 4th August and authorized yet more land to be acquired in Drummond Street, this time on the south west corner of the Melton Street junction, probably this was because it facilitated a larger station building and substation than was possible on the older site. Also authorized were powers to enter into agreements with the London & North Western Railway (L&NWR) about interconnection with the tube lines that were to run beneath the sprawling main line station. A legal agreement followed on 12th December that allowed the Hampstead Railway and C&SLR to build a low-level interconnecting passage together with a station entrance below the main line station itself; the latter was to be paid for by the L&NWR, with that company managing day-to-day operation of the lifts, entrance and booking office at their joint expense.

The common approach to the three railways was achieved by a team of six Americans who accompanied Yerkes to London and set up their headquarters at Hamilton House on the Embankment near Blackfriars (the building is still there). These specialists first arrived in 1900 and set about their task with zeal, soon surrounding themselves with a multi-national team of skilled engineers including French, Germans, Italians and Swedes (and even some English). Only the draughtsmen were stuck in the offices, the engineers were out and about as much as possible pushing the work forward and insisting on top quality workmanship. The Bakerloo was the first line to open (on 10th March 1906) as Yerkes had taken over a partially constructed line which was therefore the quickest to complete. The Piccadilly opened on 15th December 1906 (with some stations incomplete) while the Hampstead line was at last ready for opening on Saturday 22nd June 1907, though it was another week before the Hampstead formally took it over from the contractors (the UERL), suggesting it wasn't *quite* ready.

OPENING AND DESCRIPTION

The honour of opening the 'Hampstead Tube', as it was first called, fell to the Right Honourable David Lloyd George who as President of the Board of Trade in the Liberal government was the minister responsible for railways. He and a large number of guests joined a special train at Charing Cross: the train proceeded to Highgate then back to Mornington Crescent before switching over to the Golders Green branch. Once the guests had repaired to the workshops at Golders Green to enjoy a sumptuous luncheon (and to endure some lengthy speeches) the line was thrown open to the public free of charge; according to *The Railway Times* some 127,500 made use of the opportunity prior to the line closing at

8.45pm. Visitors had to obtain their free tickets from the booking offices. Opening coincided with publication of a weekly news sheet called *The Mole* which promoted the Yerkes network as a single system and advertised interesting destinations on the Hampstead Tube as places good for a visit. Prophetically, the first edition attempted (by drawing attention to the issue) to limit the confusion caused by Euston Road station being different from Euston while the Central London's Tottenham Court Road was the same as the Hampstead's Oxford Street—matters ultimately solved by renaming.

The Hampstead Tube, like the Bakerloo and Piccadilly before it, was a tremendous technical success. Reliable equipment and spacious stations now served a public whose journeys were vastly speeded up and who benefited from far better transport links between the quite remote heights of Hampstead and London's commercial zone. It was not, however, a financial success, having cost some £5m to build (much more than first planned) and during its first complete year of operation carrying some 25 million passengers, just half of that it was hoped would flock to it. While the railway could meet its loan repayments it was quite unable to pay a dividend to its shareholders, which did not augur well. The other tubes and the newly electrified District Railway were in much the same boat and UERL shareholders took the drastic steps of beefing up its management, financial reconstruction, collaboration between the various separate concerns to introduce through fares and improve marketing, and some cost cutting, largely by amalgamating resource across the companies although they remained legally separate.

Yerkes had died at the end of 1905, just when his plans had begun to unravel; his place as Chairman was taken by financier Edgar Speyer but day-to-day business was soon put into the hands of Sir George Stegmann Gibb, previously general manager of the North Eastern Railway who approached the ailing UERL with a range of modern management methods that had served him well in his previous job. He was soon joined by a number of new managers, including Frank Pick (also from the North Eastern), and a successful young manager from New Jersey, Albert Stanley, who was recruited after pressure had been exerted by concerned

THE MOLE

Published Weekly

" Well said, old Mole ! canst work i' the earth so fast?
A worthy pioneer !"—Hamlet, Act I., Scene 5.

Series A   SATURDAY, June 29, 1907.   No. 2

Opening of the Hampstead Tube.

By invitation of the Charing Cross, Euston and Hampstead Railway Company, many thousands of Londoners saw Golder's Green for the first time last Saturday. It was a happy thought to celebrate the inauguration of the line by throwing it open to the public; indeed, such an incident is characteristic of the attitude which the Underground Electric Railways Company has taken from its commencement. Everything which might conduce to the comfort and convenience of the travelling public has been thought of, planned, and carried out at an enormous expense ; and having completed its work, the Company said, " Come and see for yourselves." Over 130,000 passengers came and saw during the seven hours which the line was open last Saturday. The glorious heath of Hampstead was the quest of many, but the majority went right through to the terminus at Golder's Green, where the trains emerge into the open amidst some of the most beautiful scenery in the home counties. The sudden burst from the bowels of the earth into the sunlit fields seemed to reveal like a flash the purpose of it all. Half-an-hour suffices to transport the London toiler from the " hub of the universe " to the waving meadows of the golden hill. " Live in the Country " has been the catchword for many a month, but how ? In one direction, at least, the Hampstead Tube has solved the problem.

Formal Inauguration.

Prior to the inauguration of public traffic on the Hampstead Tube, the line was declared open with all due pomp and circumstance by Mr. Lloyd George, President of the Board of Trade. Armed with a massive gold spanner (the appearance of which so soon after the disappearance of the Ascot Cup did not fail to arouse suspicion), he switched on the current through the motorman's controller, and the train sped away northward from Charing Cross. After proceeding to the Highgate terminus, the train returned thence to the junction at Camden Town, and afterwards went on to the other terminus at Golder's Green. At a luncheon which followed in the car sheds, interesting speeches were made by Sir George Gibb, Sir Edgar Speyer, and Mr. Lloyd George, M.P. Sir George Gibb, who is the Chairman of the Hampstead Tube, said that this was, in some ways, the most important of the railways constructed by the Underground Electric Railways Company of London, in that it opened up

Hampstead and Highgate, to which access had hitherto been somewhat inconvenient, and thus provided the people of London with new possibilities of living in the country. He also made the welcome announcement that arrangements had practically been concluded for through fares with the Central London Railway. Sir Edgar Speyer, the Chairman of the Underground Electric Railways Company of London, who followed, pointed out that the tubes built by that company would save vast outlays in connexion with the widening and maintenance of streets, and in relieving the congestion of traffic would be the means of saving time to the users not only of the tubes themselves, but also of the streets. Mr. Lloyd-George congratulated all concerned on the opening of the last of the series of tube railways, and said he had been glad to read the report of the Board of Trade Inspector, who spoke in the highest terms about the railway, both from the engineering point of view and from that of the comfort and security of the public. It was a wonder how London could have got on without its underground railways, which last year carried over 240,000,000 passengers. Even so, the streets were congested enough; but what would have happened without the tubes? More than that, Sir Edgar Speyer and those who collaborated with him had done more to assist in solving the housing problem in London than the most skilfully devised Act of Parliament could do.

WHERE TO GO

EVENTS of the WEEK.	Date.	HOW they may be reached.
BALKAN STATES EXHIBITION at Earl's Court	May to October	Through tickets issued from all Tube Stations including entrance to the Exhibition.
SUNDAY CONCERTS at Royal Albert Hall	Every Sunday	Book to South Kensington (Piccadilly Tube).
SUNDAY CONCERTS at Queen's Hall	Every Sunday	Book to Oxford Circus (Bakerloo Tube).
PALESTINE EXHIBITION at Agricultural Hall	Daily to July 2nd	Book to Angel (via King's Cross)
M.C.C. v. OXFORD UNIVERSITY ... At Lord's	June 29th	Book to Baker Street (Bakerloo Tube).
SURREY v. WARWICKSHIRE ... At the Oval	June 29th	Book through to Oval.
GREAT GALA DAY & GRAND DISPLAY OF FIREWORKS at Alexandra Palace	June 29th	Book through to Alexandra Palace (G.N.R.) via Piccadilly Tube.
TONIC SOL-FA CHOIR FÉTE at Crystal Palace	June 29th	Book to Elephant and Castle via Bakerloo Tube, and thence to Crystal Palace via S.E. & C.Rly.
ENGLAND v. SOUTH AFRICA at Lord's	July 1st—3rd	Book to Baker Street (Bakerloo Tube).
OXFORD v. CAMBRIDGE at Lord's...	July 4th—6th	Book to Baker Street (Bakerloo Tube.
BUSINESS EXHIBITION at Olympia	July 4th to 13th	Book to Barons Court or Olympia.

First two pages from Issue 2 of *The Mole*, which reported the opening of the Hampstead Tube. The previous week's issue (launched on the opening day) was fulsome in its description of the new Tube's facilities and the districts it served. It was made available at stations on all the Yerkes lines.

This carefully posed view shows one of the Hampstead's new trains at the crossover tunnel at Hampstead itself, control trailer car leading. At this time control trailer cabs offered very little protection for the driver. The image is also useful in showing the track and electrification equipment.

American stockholders (although Stanley made his mark in America he was actually English and in 1920 was created 1st Baron Ashfield). The new team vigorously promoted the District and the tubes as a single network and during 1908 obtained agreement from the independent underground railways to promote the entire network under the name UNDERGROUND—this logotype being applied to signs at each station and to common publicity such as maps (see illustration in the colour section at the beginning of this book). This was an extension of a consensus agreed the previous year for the independents to work together for their mutual benefit, and while difficulties soon arose the UNDERGROUND formula endured for another half century and with this successful recipe traffic began to pick up. In 1909 Hampstead passengers numbered nearly 30 million and the railway could afford a modest 3/4 per cent dividend.

With effect from 1st July 1910 the formal amalgamation of the Yerkes tubes was achieved by means of an Act of Parliament. The mechanics were that the statutory title of the Great Northern, Piccadilly & Brompton Railway was altered to the London Electric Railway (LER) and at the same time it absorbed the Charing Cross, Euston & Hampstead and the Baker Street & Waterloo Railways which from that point on were managed as a single concern. The lines remained physically separate and were therefore referred to as the Piccadilly, Hampstead and Bakerloo Lines respectively. Albert Stanley became managing director of the LER and had also just become managing director of the UERL upon Gibb's departure to the new Road Board.

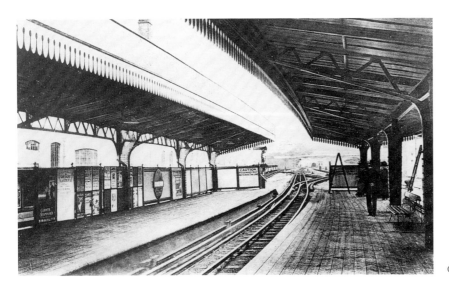

Golders Green, looking south from the departure platform shortly after line opening.

The LER soon set about improving the network in response to the unequal building up of traffic that was beginning to choke the system at a number of pinch points. One of these was Charing Cross where the Hampstead Line terminated under the main line station but did not connect with the nearby District or Bakerloo Lines. To remedy this an Act was obtained in 1910 to extend the Hampstead to a single new platform underneath the District station at Charing Cross; the platform was to be situated on a loop line that eliminated the need for the driver to walk from one end of the train to the other at this end of the journey (the alignment was slightly changed by another Act in 1911). At the same time Charing Cross (District) station was entirely reconstructed and equipped with four escalators—these first made their appearance at Earls Court in 1911 so the decision to adopt this modern feature in advance of the Earls Court test was forward-looking, to say the least. The escalators only rose to the level under the District platforms and the street couldn't be reached entirely by escalators until 1928. Work began in October 1911 and the new Hampstead platform and escalators came into service on 6th April 1914; the Bakerloo escalators had already come into service on 2nd March but reconstruction of the old surface building was not completed until the end of the year—its external appearance is substantially unchanged today.

Parts of the loop were exceedingly sharp and some minor modifications were required to the rolling stock to prevent the cars fouling the tunnel walls. The extension gave rise to two adjacent stations potentially having the same name, which was clearly undesirable. At first the older Hampstead station was renamed Charing Cross (Strand), and the new platform Charing Cross (Embankment). This was evidently found unsatisfactory and the former station was simply renamed Strand on 9th May 1915 and at the new station the Embankment suffix was dropped at the same time. This already confusing position was compounded by further renaming in the 1970s when the arrival of the new Jubilee Line at Strand caused a similar process to be carried out, this time in reverse. Thus 'Strand' reverted to its original name of Charing Cross while the station down by the river is now called Embankment.

This view of Edgware station, looking south, was taken shortly after opening in 1924 and shows the two covered platforms connected to the large station building with the car sheds on the left and four more covered sidings on the extreme left. A bus garage nestles behind the station. The proposed line of the Watford & Edgware railway is visible in the left foreground (with bridging for the shops and service road provided). The Great Northern Railway's Edgware branch can be seen in the distance, crossing the Hampstead Line. The rural nature of the area is striking.

AND ON TO HENDON AND EDGWARE

While the CCE&HR was evolving at the dawn of the twentieth century another scheme was emerging that proposed an independent line connecting the Hampstead with the villages of Hendon and Edgware, then somewhat remote and agricultural. The result was a proposed Edgware & Hampstead Railway (E&HR) and during 1901 it was planned to join the CCE&HR end-on, immediately north of Hampstead station, where through operation

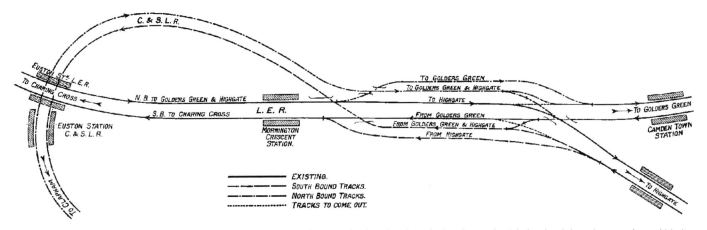

This schematic diagram shows the complex post-1924 arrangements at Camden Town; the dotted tracks at the junctions at the right hand end show the route along which the original Highgate and Hampstead branches converged.

was apparently contemplated. The bill received the Royal Assent on 18th November 1902 but by this time plans had changed, with the Hampstead Railway itself planning to serve Golders Green where an end on junction was negotiated with the E&HR, which Yerkes offered to take over and construct himself. Although the control of the E&HR came under UERL influence it was not the most pressing work to undertake and activity was confined to realigning the route to avoid emerging housing development near Golders Green; it was not until 1912 that powers were taken for the company to be taken over by the LER as a prelude to construction. These powers also authorized some deviations to the route, including a new alignment between Golders Green and Hendon. Another company, the Watford & Edgware Railway, was formed in 1903 with powers to build a line from Watford to an end on junction with the E&HR; after a while this company also came under the UERL influence but work never got going and the powers lapsed in 1909.

During 1913 most of the land required for an extension to Edgware had been purchased but just as fencing began the First World War broke out and it was not practicable to continue. After the war the extension was seen as a reasonably high priority but money was now short and it was not possible to raise capital until 1922 in consequence of the government passing the Trade Facilities Act, which offered a government guarantee for approved public works, in turn reducing borrowing costs. The extension (being an approved work) could now proceed: Charles Brand was awarded the Golders Green–Hendon section, and the Foundation Company the section to Edgware. Most of the extension was in open air though there was a half-mile tunnel through the ridge immediately north of Hendon (this was originally to have been deep cutting), beyond which the ground was relatively level. Between Golders Green and Hendon there were considerable lengths of steep cuttings and viaducts, including a long viaduct across the Brent valley. The extension to Hendon was opened on 19th November 1923 by Sir Philip Lloyd-Graeme, MP for Hendon and also President of the Board of Trade (though that department was no longer connected with railways). The extension to Edgware opened on 18th August 1924 and included a 4-road car shed with inspection pits (four more sidings in the open air came into use in December).

CAMDEN RECONSTRUCTION AND LINK TO C&SLR

During 1913 control of the pioneering City & South London Railway (C&SLR), together with the still-independent Central London Railway (CLR), passed to the UERL as the best way of protecting the shareholders. By then the C&SLR operated between Euston and Clapham Common, still with its diminutive locomotive-hauled trains, manually operated signalling and primitive equipment. Although even the oldest section of line had not seen a quarter-century of service the whole line desperately needed modernizing and the UERL recognized this when it took it over. It seemed attractive to connect it to the Hampstead Line, for several reasons. First it would avoid the extremely inconvenient interchange at Euston for the residents of North London wanting to go to and from the City, thereby stimulating traffic; secondly the splitting of the Hampstead Line service at Camden Town meant each northern branch was carrying far fewer trains than there was capacity, and there was therefore room for C&SLR trains to supplement the service to Highgate and Edgware. Thirdly, the C&SLR depot at Stockwell was extremely inconvenient and connection with the Hampstead would allow it to make use of Golders Green depot once new trains were put into service. For this to work it would be necessary for complicated junctions at Camden Town to be constructed to avoid conflicting movements. Through working of trains rather implied that a common pool of rolling stock would be required; while there is some evidence that a scaled down type of train was contemplated for operation solely within the constricted C&SLR tunnels the only satisfactory long term solution was to enlarge the old tunnels (at huge expense) and this, too, was being considered when war broke out.

After the war the Trade Facilities Act finally allowed a start to be made. The saga of the enlargement of the C&SLR tunnels is not really part of this story, suffice to say the line between Euston and Moorgate closed for reconstruction on 9th August 1922 and (following a serious accident) the rest of the line was closed from 28th November 1923. In the meantime work began on the Camden Town junctions and the new link line (built by the LER) which connected Camden Town with the C&SLR station at Euston. The works at Camden Town were incredibly complicated. They involved shifting the existing splitting points for the Hampstead and Highgate branches about 700 feet farther south and threading the new link from Euston C&SLR in between the relocated branch tunnels, together with new junctions that threw off connections to either branch. For some distance there were to be six parallel tracks rising or falling prior to some lines crossing over others. Mowlem's were the main contractors and operated from two shafts near Mornington Crescent and another at Ampthill Square, and six Greathead shields removed 80,000 tons of soil.

The new link and some of the enlarged railway came into service on 20th April 1924 (Easter Day) when through trains began operating between Hendon Central (later Edgware) and Moorgate, and from 1st December 1924 when trains were projected from Moorgate to the southern terminus at Clapham Common. Today's Northern Line began to take shape.

INDUSTRIAL TROUBLES

After the First World War there was considerable industrial unrest, some general and some especially affecting the railway industry. Coal industry problems caused a succession of fuel shortages from 1918 resulting in some stations temporarily closing early or on Sundays with train services being scaled back. A railway strike from 27th September 1919 saw much of the Underground closed. Across the network over 5000 volunteers were enrolled and hastily trained and it was even found possible to stoke up the power house—the Hampstead Line managed to operate a Golders Green–Charing Cross service from 30th September and even resumed a service to Highgate from 4th October, though all stations had reopened on 6th and normal services resumed quickly thereafter. Further unrest in the coal industry caused serious difficulty during 1921, and from 1st August stations were opened an hour later and closed an hour earlier to save fuel; this was eased a little towards the end of the year but left the network operating slightly fewer hours than previously. Unrest flared up again from January 1924. This reached serious proportions when a strike of workers at the power house between 5th and 12th June disrupted services by drastically reduced power output, but it allowed services of a sort to continue although many stations were closed.

THE TALE OF MR. BRACKETT

The editor of the Underground's staff magazine was moved to recall the occasion when a passenger reputedly alighted from a train after South Kentish Town closed (it is noted that it was not always possible to staff all gangways along a train, so it is not inconceivable the event occurred).

(Editor's Note :—Soon after South Kentish Town Station was closed to traffic a train stopped there and a man absentmindedly alighted. The train departed and he had to be collected by a later train. The following verses are, of course, purely imaginative and are illustrated by MR. F. H. STINGEMORE.*)*

THE train to Highgate opened, Mr. Brackett stepped without,
He struck a match to light his pipe—a
" zephyr " blew it out,
" 'Tis strange " said Mr. Brackett, as the train left him behind,
" How very dark this station is —Good gracious! Am I blind ! "

He lit another match and by its feeble little flame,
He made out " Benedictine " ; then he saw the station name !
" Whatever shall I do ? " he said, and shouted down the track,

But no one heard the question and an echo sent it back.
Then came a distant rumble, and another train swept by,
Poor Brackett waved and shouted, but it never heard him " Hi,"
And 'till the close of traffic rushing " Highgates " came and went,
When Brackett fell asleep against a barrel of cement.

★　　★　　★

When morning came he started on his hands and knees to crawl,
And made a lot of progress 'till his forehead hit a wall.
Then he sat and chewed a poster which was advertising " Port,"
But the paste upon it proved a most unsatisfying sort.
All day upon the platform Mr. Brackett sat and fumed,
His mind was full of pictures—of the day he'd be exhumed ;

His widow and his orphans, and the story in the Press,
His mystified employers—was there ever such a mess !
" I cannot stand it longer . . . I will run to Kentish Town,
I'll risk electrocution " . . . to the rails he clambered down.
But scarcely had he taken eighteen paces down the line,
When red lights changed to green—and Brackett scurried back in " nine " !

★   ★   ★

Four days have now elapsed since Mr. Brackett disappeared,
His wife would never know him with his funny little beard.
The sympathetic neighbours have expressed their deepest woe,
And whispered to each other " Yes, I often thought he'd go ! "
From Portland Place and Fleet Street, now, the news begins to pour,
Photographers' magnesium lies thick upon the floor.
Police have cross-examined Mrs. B., and asked her straight,
" What sort of husband was he ? Was he early ? Was he late ? "

★   ★   ★

One day as Mr. Brackett sat upon the spiral stairs,
A circumstance occurred which threw a light upon affairs,
A circumstance which proved to be the greatest piece of luck,
A match, deep in the lining of his coat . . . a match, *unstruck* !
He hastened to the platform, screwed some posters in a ball,
And in between the cyclones, struck the match upon a wall.
His eyes were nearly blinded after seven darksome days,
But the next oncoming motorman espied the bonfire's blaze !

★   ★   ★

So ends the tale of Brackett, there is little left to tell,
Not only is he still alive, but happy, fit and well.
The Company, moreover, waived their claim to seal his fate
" *For being on the premises with ' Season ' out of date.*"

T. W.

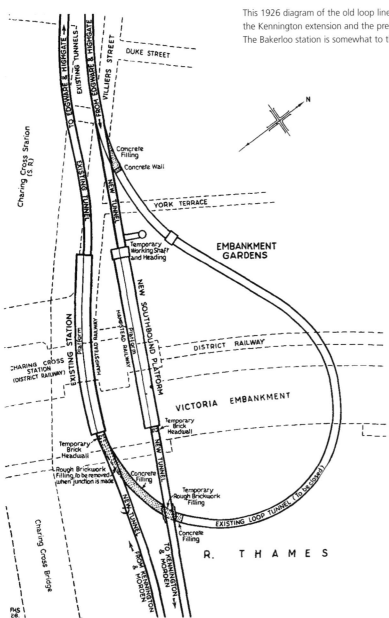

This 1926 diagram of the old loop line at Charing Cross shows its relationship to the tracks along the Kennington extension and the present day station. The 1914 platform is the one on the left. The Bakerloo station is somewhat to the left of these structures and is not shown here.

These mainly returned to use from 12th June (with normal train services from 14th) but Mornington Crescent only re-opened from 2nd July and the decision was taken not to re-open South Kentish Town at all—the last train calling during the morning of 5th June. In 1926 the general strike broke out on 4th May in sympathy with the lock out of the miners and stopped nearly all services on the Underground except for a few trains on the Central London. Again, volunteers were enrolled although naval ratings were despatched to the power house this time. Skeleton services were introduced on other lines (including the Hampstead) from 7th and 8th May and gradually it became possible to get a third of the train service operating; normal service resumed from 15th May. During the strike the numbers of volunteers rose to 9600 and passengers were carried at a flat fare of 3d.

The closure of South Kentish Town allowed services to be slightly accelerated and while the lifts were removed and a large ventilation fan later installed the platforms survived intact until 1936 when they were demolished. The station saw use as a shelter during the Second World War requiring the tracks to be separated from the shelter by a massive new wall, demolished with some effort soon after hostilities ended. The station building survives.

To Kennington

During the early 1920s the UERL decided to extend the C&SLR to Morden and Sutton to make better use of that line's capacity and to open up new districts. As part of the same programme of works it was considered desirable to extend the Hampstead's terminus southwards from Charing Cross (where there was surplus capacity) to connect with poorly-served Waterloo and then to meet the C&SLR at Kennington where it could pick up some of the West End traffic from the Morden extension. The terminal loop at Charing Cross would have to be abandoned but a new loop was to be constructed at Kennington and a proportion of the Hampstead's service would use this to reverse, the remaining proportion would cross over to the C&SLR south of the station. As part of this programme another Camden Town type junction complex was planned at Waterloo connecting with the Bakerloo; the junction would allow Hampstead Line trains from the north to proceed either towards Kennington or Elephant & Castle (Bakerloo) with corresponding options for southbound Bakerloo trains, and with northbound trains from Elephant & Castle or Kennington each able to proceed towards Tottenham Court Road or Oxford Circus. It is perhaps for the best that the Southern Railway's desire to protect its interests saw this scheme withdrawn during the parliamentary process and the C&SLR bottled up at Morden, with the Southern building the proposed line to Sutton. A reversing siding was planned south of Waterloo recognising the heavy flows Waterloo itself would generate, but before construction started the siding was shifted to a point south of Kennington where it was accommodated with some difficulty.

Work on the LER's Kennington extension began on 22nd April 1924 by the Metropolitan Tunnel & Public Works Company with tunnelling faces fed by via a number of worksites including Embankment Gardens, Lambeth North and Kennington Park. The works at Charing Cross were complicated by the need for the new southbound line to pierce the existing reversing loop which meant it had to be taken out of use and sealed up in advance of the extension. To maintain a train service to the busy platform at Charing Cross, from 25th January 1926 all Edgware branch trains used the northbound platform at Strand and then worked to Charing Cross and back on a single line basis; meanwhile all Highgate trains were reversed in Strand southbound platform. Perhaps incredibly, it was possible to maintain normal intervals north of Strand. While the works were in hand the new

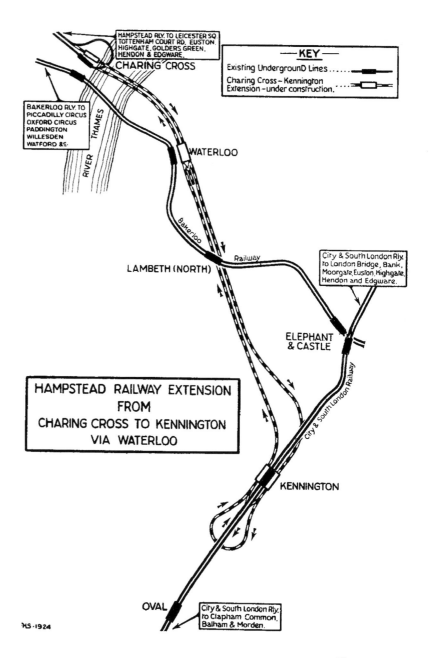

HAMPSTEAD RAILWAY EXTENSION
FROM
CHARING CROSS TO KENNINGTON
VIA WATERLOO

HS·1924

northbound line from Waterloo was plugged into the old loop platform at Charing Cross immediately south of the station and the old loop tunnel was blocked off. The link between Charing Cross and Kennington opened on 13th September 1926 (the same day the C&SLR extended to Morden).

From 1st July 1933 the London Passenger Transport Board—better known as London Transport—came into being. Under new ownership the former use of the suffix 'Railway' for the different train services was no longer appropriate: instead the word 'Line' became universal. This didn't really work with the intermingled Hampstead Line and City & South London Railway and a single new name was sought. Even before 1933 several names were attempted, and some publicity used 'Edgware, Highgate & Morden Line'. London Transport's first attempt to improve on this was the 'Edgware & Morden Line' in 1934, but—all entirely logical names having been dismissed—the happy name 'Northern Line' was selected and publicly announced on 23rd August 1937. One reason for the choice of name was that the line was to be part of widespread extension at its northern end. The Highgate branch was to be extended to East Finchley to meet the old GNR branch from Finsbury Park which was to be electrified to Finchley Central, High Barnet, Mill Hill East and Edgware; at the latter station the Northern Line trains from the Finchley direction would operate into the old Hampstead Line station and train services from that direction extended over new track to Elstree and Aldenham over the old Watford and Edgware route. These schemes are beyond the scope of this book, but it must be recorded that Highgate branch trains were extended to East Finchley on 3rd July 1938, High Barnet on 14th April 1940 and Mill Hill East on 18th May 1941, the projections to Edgware and Elstree were initially suspended during the war and later abandoned. As part of the scheme Highgate station was renamed Archway (Highgate) on 11th June 1939, with the confusing suffix dropped when a new station at Highgate opened on 19th January 1941 underneath the main line station of that name. Notwithstanding these significant later additions, the Northern Line had really taken its main shape and form from 1926 when the Morden and Kennington extensions opened.

PART TWO
THE ROUTE AND THE STATIONS

The Hampstead Line is curious in that the track level at Golders Green is elevated 272 feet higher than Charing Cross (Strand) requiring northbound trains to operate against a rising gradient almost continuously, the most severe being 1:60 most of the way north of Chalk Farm. The lay of the ground above gives rise to some other odd features. The peculiar geography means the deepest point on the Underground below surface level (221 feet below Whitestone Pond, north of Hampstead) was nevertheless about 130 feet higher than the lowest point on the Underground, on the Kennington extension, near the Thames (just south of Waterloo) where the line is only 80ft below road level. The Underground's deepest tube station is Hampstead, where rail level is 192 feet below road level, but the shallowest tube station is just down the line at Chalk Farm, only 39 feet below the pavement. Where feasible the original section of line was built under streets to avoid the need for compensating property owners. On the Highgate branch this required a tortuous route that made it difficult to get both tunnels to follow the road without extremely sharp curves, so between points south of Kentish Town and north

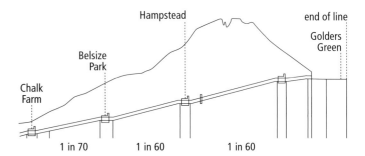

This sketch shows the relationship of the Hampstead Railway with the hilly terrain, and the need for the lengthy continuous gradient in order to surface at Golders Green.

of Tufnell Park the tunnels are sometimes one directly over the other; this gives rise to untypical station layouts at those stations where the platforms are all on the east side of the line, and at different levels. The unauthorized section between Euston and Kings Cross was also to have had such an arrangement under the narrow Church Way west of Chalton Street.

As described earlier, by the time construction work was put in hand the decision had been made to build the line on a more robust scale. The main improvements were in making the platforms 350ft long and out of concrete, and equipping the line for an even more intense train service. Station designs were pretty much standardized across all three Yerkes tubes. On the Hampstead the final list of stations are set out below; unexceptionally, there was some vacillation about the exact station names to be used and it might be helpful to list these at the same time:

Proposed or Suggested Name	Station Name at Opening
Golders Green	Golders Green
Heath Street*	Hampstead
Belsize	Belsize Park
Adelaide Road	Chalk Farm
Archway Tavern	Highgate
Tufnell Park	Tufnell Park
Kentish Town	Kentish Town
Castle Road*	South Kentish Town
Camden Road (and for a while Mother Redcap)	Camden Town
Seymour Street	Mornington Crescent
Euston	Euston
Euston Road	Euston Road
Tottenham Court Road	Tottenham Court Road
Oxford Street	Oxford Street
Cranbourn Street	Leicester Square (joint with Piccadilly)
Charing Cross	Charing Cross

* appears in tilework name at platform level

Unease about the selection of names continued even after opening and on 9th March 1908 Oxford Street became Tottenham Court Road (to agree with the Central London station with which it was connected), and the old Tottenham Court Road became Goodge Street, though it was in the middle of the former road and 100 yards from any part of the latter. Euston Road was also found to be a particularly unhelpful name and was renamed Warren Street on 7th June 1908; though there could have been few who had ever heard of the road, the station did at least have one of its entrances in it.

At surface level two storey buildings were the norm, with lift equipment and some staff accommodation on the upper floor. Stations were built using then novel steel frame construction in-filled with brick or block-work and covered with dark red glazed terra cotta blocks supplied by Leeds Fireclay, illuminated at night by powerful arc lights which made the station structures stand out. A characteristic feature was the arched windows to the upper storey. Separate ways in and out were provided, the lifts either disgorging directly into the street, or into a short passage leading to the street. The station entrance led to a ticket office and waiting area, then the way in to the lifts.

At Highgate the station entrance was in Junction Road, but a second entrance was opened in 1912 from Highgate Hill. At Oxford Street and Charing Cross great difficulty had been encountered obtaining suitable sites for surface buildings and tickets halls were consequently built below street level. At Euston the London & North Western Railway (L&NWR) was keen to have access to both the new Hampstead Railway and the City & South London Railway, which also extended to Euston in 1907. As a result the L&NWR built and equipped its own entrance underneath the main line concourse by the carriage drive between platforms 2 and 5, but using the Underground's contractors. All three railways collaborated over the operation of this ticket office and the low level interconnecting subways; the L&NWR required the Hampstead and C&SLR to maintain their own separate station entrances at Euston and until 1922 they staffed and managed the facility under their own station. Following the UERL's acquisition of the C&SLR it seemed rather wasteful to be operating three

Leicester Square station soon after opening and before the massive superstructure was built. The lift equipment, some station offices and office space to let were accommodated on the first floor, together with the companies' telephone exchange.

Tufnell Park offers another example of how this flexible format was used to provide a consistent design.

Chalk Farm ticket hall shows typical features of the Yerkes tubes, but is perhaps more spacious than some. The ticket office is on the left, with lifts in the background and steps leading to the basement (where they connected with the circular stair shaft). A characteristic self-winding clock completes the view. Only two lifts were fitted and the woodwork to the right of the lifts protected an empty shaft.

entirely independent stations at Euston even though the agreement with the L&NWR required it. Following negotiation on this point, the Hampstead's Melton Street, and C&SLR's Seymour Street, entrances were closed from 30th September 1914, all traffic thenceforth being handled via the compact booking office under the L&NWR station, with its single set of access stairs. For some reason, presumably to improve flows, the lift entrance and exit arrangements at the top landing were reversed from 18th February 1917.

At Charing Cross one exit (which is still there) led directly into the SE&CR station. There was a separate stairway to the forecourt adjacent to Strand and a third access in a passage leading directly into Villiers Street. At Oxford Street stairwells were placed within the pavements at three street corners around the busy junction. At both of these stations, and at Euston L&NWR, the lift equipment had to be installed at the bottom of the lift shafts as there was no room above.

At low level, except for Tufnell Park and Kentish Town (already mentioned), nearly all the stations had a pair of adjacent platforms linked by common entrances, exits and other cross passages.

The main line station at Charing Cross had direct access to the Hampstead
tube via this stairway from the concourse. The connection is still there.

The new tube at Charing Cross also had a direct entrance from the Strand,
connected to the ticket hall which had been such a problem to build. The
dull rainy day on which the photograph was taken merely adds to the
mood of depression that attended this entrance until it closed in 1973.

Warren Street had side platforms, allowing the tracks to be kept
close together for the sharp curve into Drummond Street. A strict
one way flow was promoted at every station, with separate
passageways to and from the platforms and the lifts. At most
stations these passages crossed one of the platform tunnels by
means of a steel bridge, with stairs coming down between the
platforms to which they linked by cross passages (the lifts, being
under the building line, were usually offset from the platforms
under the roadway). At a few stations the access passages connected
directly into the platform ends but nearby cross passages allowed
the one way flow to be maintained.

Platform finishes were initially planned to be completed

Euston joint ticket hall in October 1927; this cramped space hardly changed between 1907 and 1967.

The main entrance to the joint ticket hall at Euston from the main line station. Taken before the First World War, the sign over the entrance shows evidence of the word 'Tube' having been obliterated.

This plan of Euston shows the relationship of the joint ticket hall and lower subways with the London & North Western, City & South London and Charing Cross, Euston & Hampstead Railways. Hard to imagine today, the joint ticket hall was a little to the north of the promenade running along the top of the access ramps in the main line circulating area, just west of platform 2. The end of the Hampstead platforms are shown at the far left.

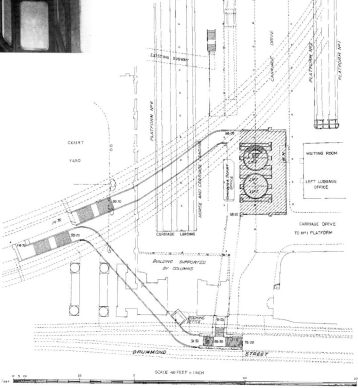

In common with the other two Yerkes tubes (the Bakerloo and Piccadilly), each of the Hampstead line stations was decorated with a unique tile pattern and colour scheme at platform level. The tiles measured 9 x 3 inches and were fixed to the walls on the platform side up to a height of about 7ft 6ins. There was a series of vertical 'rings', 2½ tiles wide, which projected above the pattern area, over the tunnel vault and down to about head height on the track side, where they met a horizontal strip of three courses of tiles. The pattern panels were formed between the rings above waist height and ran the full length of the platforms. Most stations from Euston to Charing Cross were further enhanced by *art nouveau* Way Out and No Exit signs within some of the rings. Curiously though, the platforms still had vitreous enamelled iron direction signs, in wooden frames, screwed over the tiling. In the above illustration, the pattern was of china blue and cream.

entirely in white tilework like the Central London Railway, but Yerkes had American ideas and thought he could do better by introducing different design finishes at each station, but to a common corporate theme. As developed, each station had a basic system of characteristic coloured horizontal and vertical tilework bands on a white or cream tiled ground, but in the upper portions a geometrical tiled pattern was created in the resultant rectangular panels so that every station had a different pattern or colour combination; three panels on each platform instead bore the station name in 15-inch high letters. The coloured tiling effect on a light (usually white or cream) ground was carried through the subways and lower lift landings. Although the architect Leslie Green was responsible for the detailed designs Yerkes himself took

a close interest and initiated contact with the various tiling manufacturers; he may have been influenced by the tilework designs on the contemporary New York subway where it was felt the level of illiteracy was such that reliance purely on station name boards might not be satisfactory. At ticket hall level the designs were quite different with stations generally finished with white plastered or tiled upper parts and green tiled walls up to about shoulder level, the one separated from the other by a decorative green band (usually incorporating decorative faience tiles). Ticket office windows were also surrounded by a decorative faience design.

North End station was one included in the batch authorized in 1903 and construction work was taken in hand alongside the others. The surface building was to have been on part of the site of Wyldes Farm, at a remote spot about 200 yards east of North End Road in Hampstead Way (opposite Wildwood Road). This location was immediately outside Hampstead's boundary, a commitment having been given not to build another station in that borough north of Heath Street. Though authorized by Parliament there was some local opposition from parties suspecting it might promote unwanted residential development; plans were already in hand to lay out a grid of streets east of Hampstead Way. There was considerable delay in agreeing the details of the surface building and construction of the platform tunnels and access passages had to proceed at low level with no

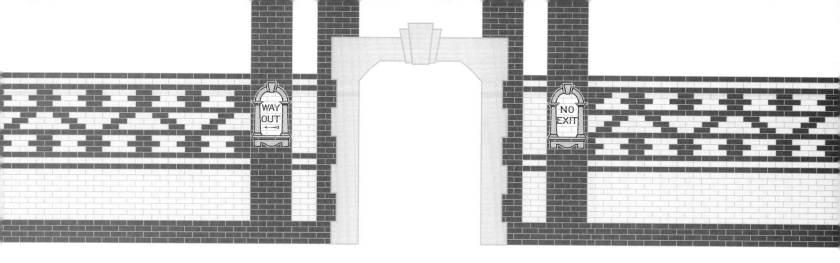

means of access to the surface, a huge inconvenience. Meanwhile, in September 1904, campaigners for preserving the character of the area succeeded in buying up a considerable quantity of land for laying out the Hampstead Heath extension, frustrating for ever much of the development potential. In April 1906, the proposed station plans were scaled down from two lift shafts (with three lifts) to one shaft (for two lifts), but still no work was done at top level. In the face of very poor prospects, the UERL finally gave up and postponed completion indefinitely with the station site lying empty and unstarted. Downstairs, the platforms were constructed, tunnel iron concreted, steps largely completed and even relevant signalling was installed (complete with platform repeating signals); but decorative finishes were omitted and the access tunnels stopped short of the intended lift landings. In 1927 part of the site was sold off to become No 1 Hampstead Way, the retained land remaining empty until a single shaft was sunk in the 1950s to an emergency control room. The platforms were demolished in the 1930s, but the space was used for secure document storage in the Second World War. The 1950s shaft proved useful in 1978 when it provided a secure means of exit for removal of some asbestos-contaminated sound-proofing panels on the southbound line as it enabled work to carry on continuously for one month without affecting traffic on the northbound line which was temporarily arranged for single line working.

Station lighting is crucial on an underground railway. Most illumination came from 'Maxim' arc lamps fed from the 600 volt lift main or (in emergency) from the track. Lower voltage dedicated lighting circuits supplied auxiliary incandescent lighting from an alternating current lighting main. In addition, each station received an independent lighting supply from the local electric light company which fed what was termed the emergency lighting circuits. These emergency lights were permanently illuminated and avoided the proposed use of gas lighting. The arrangements were necessary following new requirements of the Board of Trade that a proportion of lights be fed from an independent supply in case the main lighting failed, and about one in four lamps were so fed (there was a variety of local supply voltages along the line and staff were occasionally reminded to make sure lamps of the correct voltage were used). The arc lights had a very short life and were soon replaced by rows of incandescent lamps in characteristic hexagonal shades.

Each station had a station master's office, often at the low level formed out of a partitioned cross passage, but sometimes at basement level or in the upper station over the station entrance (with the luxury of daylight). Each was regimentally equipped with a desk and one chair, wash stand, mirror, keyboard, uniform cupboard, waste paper basket; two apron files and four lock clip files accompanied three correspondence despatch cases, a guard

FAST ELECTRIC TRAINS
FROM THIS STATION TO:-

STATION	FARE	JOURNEY TIME	STATION	FARE	JOURNEY TIME
	D	MINS		D	MINS
CHARING CROSS	1	2	TUFNELL PARK	2	13
LEICESTER SQ.	1	1	HIGHGATE	2	15
EUSTON ROAD	1	3	CHALK FARM	2	10
EUSTON	1½	4	BELSIZE PARK	2	13
CAMDEN TOWN	1½	8	HAMPSTEAD	3	16
KENTISH TOWN	2	11	GOLDERS GREEN	3	22

CONTINUOUS SERVICE

There was no surface building at Oxford Street and this is one of three stairwells that provided access to the ticket hall underneath the roadway. The photograph was taken soon after the line opened and looks north along Tottenham Court Road.

book for circulars, three (!) shoe brushes, two tri-colour lamps (one always burning), one yard of lamp wick, one clothes brush and one hair brush and comb. The Men's mess-room was equipped merely with a nest of lockers, mess table, green baize notice-board in a glazed, padlocked case, and a 5-inch gas ring with that all-important 2-quart kettle (the stationmaster also got a telephone instrument, but not his own tea-making facility). Booking offices had a gas ring for a kettle, but staff were forbidden to cook food on it. The public had no special waiting rooms but gents and ladies toilets were provided, with requisite facilities—gentlemen had 'Sunlight' soap for their use whilst ladies were able to enjoy the emollient benefits of 'Brown Windsor' soap (reputed to be Queen Victoria's favourite, but definitely made by Price & Gosnell who held royal appointment). Passengers also had access to 'literature boxes' containing the latest free maps and publicity—a bit like today's racks re-invented in the 1990s. The weekly news-sheet *The Mole* could be obtained from these.

Ticket offices each had cloakroom facilities for leaving luggage, for a fee, but with a few exceptions this arrangement did not have a very long life and by February 1909 the only remaining cloakrooms were at Charing Cross, Tottenham Court Road (previously Oxford Street), Highgate, Hampstead and Golders Green. At first a 'warehousing' charge was levied for items left for days at a time, though for some reason Sundays were not counted. Offices except Golders Green had to take bicycles (for 4d a day each), which must have been a nuisance in the tiny rooms; at Golders Green cycle racks were generously provided free. Each booking office also had a telephone extension from the stationmaster's office, though quite quickly these were adjusted to take one of the two station exchange lines, presumably to avoid unnecessarily disturbing the station master. Telephone lines were connected to the Hampstead Line's internal telephone exchange at Leicester Square but direct lines to local substations and adjacent stations were also provided, the latter via bare wires in the tunnels so that drivers stranded in the tunnels could communicate in emergencies to the adjacent stations by means of a cab-mounted telephone instrument which could be clipped onto the lines via special fly-leads. Thrift was sought from the start: orders for stores were carefully checked and issued against periodic requisition and various spent items had to be returned before replacements were forthcoming—used electric lamp globes had to be broken and glass disposed of, but the metal caps had to be returned before new lamps were issued (lamps, incidentally, were all 8 candlepower except over stairways where double power lamps were fitted). Stores were delivered from Lillie Bridge (Piccadilly) depot by road van to Goodge Street (the station called Tottenham Court Road, when opened) and Mornington Crescent, and delivered to the remaining Hampstead stations by local arrangement. It is noteworthy that the exchange telephone system lasted until 1939 when an innovative automatic system was installed.

Stations were initially supplied reasonably well with staff, though poor traffic returns meant that posts found to be unnecessary were withdrawn quite quickly. Not all stations had dedicated stationmasters, some shared stations, leaving foremen or assistant stationmasters in charge. Although conditions were quite good, leave was not generous. Stationmasters received only eight days annual leave, senior clerks six days, junior booking clerks and ticket examiners five days, ticket collectors and signalmen four days and porters and lift operators just three days leave (and that was after 12 month's satisfactory service). To modern readers it may jar that the maximum leave of 10 days was granted to travelling ticket inspectors and telephone operators. No more than one person at a station could take leave at a time, and where conflicts arose preference went to the longer serving staff. By 1928 conditions had naturally improved: the lower four classes of stationmaster got 12 days leave with pay (and the higher two classes 15 days), but a porter got only six days (still an improvement) while female staff were grudgingly tolerated as station cleaners and ladies' waiting room attendants and received three and six days respectively. The explosion in grades might be noted from the stationmaster example where there were no less than six classes; by this time assistant stationmasters had been renamed station inspectors (also six classes). The Hampstead Line had a small number of police constables from the start, though resources were quite quickly pooled with the other UERL lines to improve efficiency.

The three stairwells at Oxford Street station, seen a little later in 1914. The view this time looks south, towards Charing Cross.

Pay was reasonable in the circumstances. The basic day was of 10 hours ($9\frac{1}{2}$ for motormen) and varied from 7s 1d for a grade 1 motorman (there were five grades), 4s 6d for a booking clerk or guard, 3s 8d for a gateman and 2s 10d for a porter. A driver's pay equated with skilled manual worker of the time but a porter compared with an agricultural labourer. By the late 1920s pay rates had at least doubled, with some of the lower grades catching up a bit. As with the Metropolitan Police, constables were paid more for each year of service. Discipline was strict from the start.

The booking hall at Hampstead showing the entrance to the lifts in the 1920s. Hampstead was one of the few stations to retain cloak rooms.

Staff caught reading or sitting whilst on duty, or who were late, could expect to be suspended; a ticket collector mishandling lost property (which was supposed to be sent to the lost property office at Piccadilly Circus) could be reduced to porter or dismissed. A liftman 'operating a bad lift service' could be reduced to gateman on the trains, and a booking clerk caught smoking or anyone caught gambling could expect to be discharged.

Payment of staff was of course in cash; the arrangements varied over time but from March 1908 the three Yerkes tubes paid their staff on different days, Hampstead staff getting paid on Wednesdays each week. Initially staff at each station were paid in sequence starting at 10am at Charing Cross and finishing at 12.45pm at Golders Green, presumably by travelling paymaster— at most stations just ten minutes was allowed. Starting time was shifted to 11am at Charing Cross from March 1908, and Golders Green payment period vastly increased to allow for central payment of sundry relief staff. At first a weekly time-book was kept but the payment regime was revised to require timesheets to be completed daily and signed by each member of staff; these were forwarded to the general timekeeper at Hammersmith (Piccadilly) station before 9am each day so the daily records could be kept straight across the three tubes.

Station staff had many duties, of which cleaning was a major function. Most surface cleaning had to be done once a fortnight, but floors needed doing twice daily, platform and subway tiling daily, surface level tiling and glazing (interior and exterior) twice a week, most lighting except arc lamps twice a week (more frequently on stairs). A lesser regime applied to higher level surfaces and inaccessible areas were dealt with by engineering staff. Cleaning was a perfectly normal part of the station staff regime until the 1980s during which decade it was gradually shifted to external cleaning contractors.

The initial disposition of lifts was two each at Tufnell Park, Kentish Town, South Kentish Town, Chalk Farm, Mornington Crescent and Euston (Melton Street entrance); three lifts each at Highgate, Belsize Park, Camden Town, Euston (Interchange); four lifts each at Euston Road (now Warren Street), Tottenham Court Road (now Goodge Street), Oxford Street (now Tottenham Court Road), and Charing Cross (later Strand). By variation to the original plan, both Hampstead and Leicester Square had five lifts, the latter being shared with the Piccadilly Line. Leicester square was odder that the fifth lift was added very much as an afterthought and had its own small shaft, the only occasion where this was done. The number of lifts required was a function both of the traffic thought likely and the cycling time of each lift (which increased in double the proportion to the depth of the shaft). The Hampstead Railway decided very quickly that the disposition of lifts was inadequate and by December 1909 additional lifts had been provided one each at Highgate and Belsize Park (now four), and Tufnell Park and Kentish Town (now three). At a few stations lifts were also removed as traffic levels rendered supply too great and the equipment was redeployed elsewhere (either another

station on the LER or in replacement of less satisfactory lifts elsewhere, such as the City & South London Railway). By 1914, Warren Street had lost one lift and Goodge Street two, and during the 1920s a lift was also removed at Tufnell Park; the vacated Goodge Street shaft was converted into a ventilation shaft.

The lifts were supplied by the Otis Elevator Company and were operated by huge, electrically operated winding gear, usually at first floor level but necessarily at the bottom of the shafts where there was no station building. The lifts each had a nominal capacity of 70 (later reduced to 50 by fitting seats) and had a trapezoid cross section that made the most efficient use of the half-shaft each lift occupied. The car gates were of the sliding lattice type. The entrance gates were opened and closed manually by the lift operator, stationed at his adjacent control position; the gates were mechanically locked closed while the lift was between landings. The exit gates were controlled by a compressed air motor actuated by a lever at the lift operator's position, and the lift was prevented from moving unless the gate was closed. At the top landing (only) each of the landing gates comprised a pair of mechanically-connected wooden sliding doors, air operated on the exit side (so these doors sometimes separated the lift directly from the street), locked unless a lift were at the landing. The arrangements were quite complex in that an air supply was required to the lift since the lift car exit gates were operated by direct action of the operator's air valve, but the landing gates had to be electrically actuated by contacts on the same lever, all having to be connected via flexible cables and air lines. Each lift also had a third means of access via a discrete door in the long edge—if a lift failed in the shaft the adjacent lift could be brought alongside and passengers transferred via these emergency doors, which were of course usually firmly locked. Lifts could also be wound (slowly) by hand if the power failed.

Following experiments on other lines many lifts on the Hampstead Line were modified in the 1920s to be capable of operation from landing level; this was useful in that a single member of staff at both top and bottom could operate several lifts and deal with ticket checking, saving staff. A certain amount of additional equipment was required, and entrance gates were

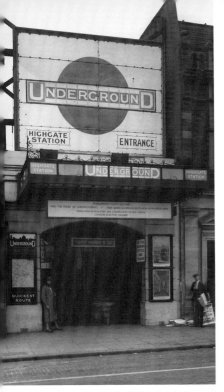

These views show the 1912-origin Highgate Hill entrance to Highgate station (today's Archway) before and after reconstruction in 1932.

automatically as a train departed from the previous station and lift operators were commanded to send a lift down as soon as the bell was heard so that passengers had time to reach the platform immediately before the train arrived.

During 1928 some experiments were put in hand at Warren Street to automate the lift service, a matter which was reasonably straightforward with lift equipment already converted for landing control. The experiment did not last very long and a more fully developed system was introduced at Earls Court in 1932 using some of the Warren Street equipment. Three of the four lifts at Strand were arranged for automatic working in May 1935. When switched on, an automatic timing system regulated their operation to provide a frequent and regular service and this was connected with a system of visual warnings indicating which lift was next to depart and when the respective sets of gates were about to close. In addition an audible warning 'Stand Clear of the Gates' was made via loudspeakers next to the relevant gates. The announcement was read by a photo-electric cell from a sound track printed on a revolving glass disk; the message at first ended with a 'please' but this was soon found unhelpful and was obliterated, leaving a pronounced crackle instead. With all three lifts in operation a 37-second service could be provided. The next development was at Goodge Street when three new fully automatic lifts came into service on 4th March 1937. These tiny lifts, built and equipped by Otis, were installed in the empty lift shaft, leaving the two older Otis lifts available for use as required. The new lifts were very unusual in having inner car doors which opened in an arc into the lift car itself. Operating at up to 600ft per minute they were the fastest lifts on the Underground at the time and offered a 34-second peak service though only holding 17 people each. Two high-speed lifts were also installed at Hampstead in 1954, this time replacing two originals. The new automatic lifts operated at 800 feet a minute and significantly reduced the transit time.

At first, station entrances and exits could be closed off by huge metal roller blinds that could be pulled down across the openings, but by the early 1920s these had been replaced by metal lattice (Bostwick) gates that slid across the openings horizontally. Many stations were quite quiet at certain times of the day, and sometimes

altered to power operation, but the system proved quite reliable, being first deployed on the Hampstead Line at Warren Street (three lifts only) in 1916 and by March 1917 the facility had also been rolled out to Highgate, Leicester Square and Strand (three lifts only), with some others following. These unmanned lifts also received an emergency lighting supply as there was no lift operator to light the emergency candle lamps in the event of power failure. The lifts at Belsize Park were never altered to landing control and remained in their original mode of operation until they were replaced in 1987. In an attempt to try and operate an ideal lift service special bells were provided in the ticket halls at stations north of Camden Town (exclusive); the bells were operated all day. At these places it was often decided to handle all the traffic through the booking hall and keep the designated lift exit closed at the top. The exact arrangements altered from time to time, but in 1926 the lift exit at Chalk Farm was designated as permanently closed, while Hampstead, Tufnell Park, Kentish Town, Mornington Crescent, Goodge Street and Strand were designated as closed 'all day'; the distinction between these two implies the exit at Chalk Farm could physically no longer be used (still the situation today). Highgate, Warren Street and Leicester Square exits were only available in the evening peaks, while at Hampstead the lift entrance at the lower landing could be used as an exit during the morning peak, probably as a means of clearing the lifts faster. Most stations had a stair shaft with a single stairway in it (not the intended double-spiral) but at Euston (interchange) and Charing Cross the stairs occupied one half of a lift shaft, the other half shaft being empty at Charing Cross, allowing a ventilation duct to be put in it.

At many stations lifts were replaced by escalators when they were reconstructed to cater for higher traffic levels and improved interchange. Six of the Hampstead's fifteen stations were reconstructed before the Second World War. The first station to receive attention was busy Tottenham Court Road where the awkward layout was quite unable to cope. Two flights of escalators were installed, the upper flight of three machines leading to an intermediate concourse from which steps led directly to the Central Line. A lower flight of two machines led to the end of the old lift landings from which the old steps led to the platforms. The lower flight and the descending escalator in the upper one came into use on 29th September 1925 enabling some of the lifts to be withdrawn; the other two escalators replaced the remaining lifts from 1st February 1926. It was extremely difficult work as the escalators emerged in the same cramped sub-surface ticket hall already occupied by the lifts, which could not be dismantled until the escalators were in use. The old street entrances were retained (though later somewhat altered) and a new passage led to the Central London Railway (CLR) station entrance providing communication with the south west corner of the road junction—the CLR station building and lifts were closed. Ventilation plant

Two of the three high speed automatic lifts introduced at Goodge Street in March 1937. Just visible inside the entrance are the lift car doors which sweep back though a right angle into the car, like some doors on modern buses.

was soon installed in some of the vacant shafts and the old Hampstead Railway emergency stairs were retained but with new passage from the ticket hall that bridged the old lift-shafts.

Camden Town, Highgate and Kentish Town station followed respectively from 7th October 1929, 15th June 1931 and 21st November 1932; in each case two escalators replaced all the lifts, again with the old stairs and station buildings retained. At Camden Town new interchange passages were introduced at the same time, slightly improving connection between Highgate and Hampstead branches. At Camden Town and Kentish Town the old station exteriors were little altered during the rebuilding. At Highgate (now Archway), the later Highgate Hill entrance was enlarged and reconstructed in modern style with stone finishes but the Junction Road façade was retained; both entrances were completely swallowed up during 1970s building development.

Warren Street followed from 27th September 1933 and offers a useful example of an awkward conundrum. It is desirable where convenient to use the existing station building when installing escalators; the latter, however go down at a slant, while the lifts they replace fall vertically. At deep stations like Warren Street this would ordinarily displace the bottom of the escalators a long way from the lift landings and platforms. The solution here was to install two flights of escalators with the lower one turned around 180 degrees bringing the lowest landing back closer to the platforms; such layouts require careful station operation to ensure escalators do not deliver people to the confined intermediate landing faster than the next flight can take them away. Although only two escalators were installed in each flight, a fixed stairway was provided between them so it was not necessary to keep the old spiral stairs (which tended to set the pattern for future station reconstruction). In the 1960s the intermediate landing proved a convenient point to plug in the Victoria Line and a third escalator was installed in the upper flight at the same time. The station had an entirely new frontage to Tottenham Court Road consisting of a single storey drum also offering some presence in Warren Street and Euston Roads, but the escalators disappeared beneath the old station piercing one of the old shafts; the old frontages to Warren Street and Euston Road were subsequently rebuilt and disappeared. The new entrance was in the prevailing new style with Portland stone external finishes and cream tiling inside.

The final station to be rebuilt before the Second World War was Leicester Square where an entirely new ticket hall was built under the road intersection with separate flights of three escalators serving the Hampstead and Piccadilly Lines. Attempts had been made in 1925 to improve the lift service at this difficult site by increasing the speed from 180 to 290ft per minute, vastly improving the service that could be offered by the main bank of four lifts (the fifth lift in its own shaft seems to have disappeared around this time); in the end complete reconstruction was the only means of further increasing capacity. Several new entrances were provided within the building line into the new ticket hall (the streets were not wide enough for independent stairwells like those at Piccadilly Circus), including two from within the old building frontage. Three new entrances were built at the corner of Little Newport street and from the frontage of the Hippodrome building, on the west side of Charing Cross Road), and the third on the east side next to Cranbourn Street. The new entrances were clad in Portland stone which also appeared within the arches of the old station. The new ticket hall came into use from 4th May 1935 though the entrances from the old building followed a month later when the lifts had been taken out; the vacated space on the ground floor of the old station was converted to lucrative retail use. The remainder of the building remained in Underground control and currently houses the Northern Line HQ staff. The Little Newport Street entrance closed in the late 1980s.

Plan of the new ticket hall at Leicester Square. The old station is in the angle between the new escalators and the new ticket hall has appropriated some of the basement area.

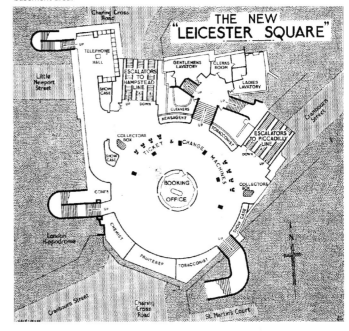

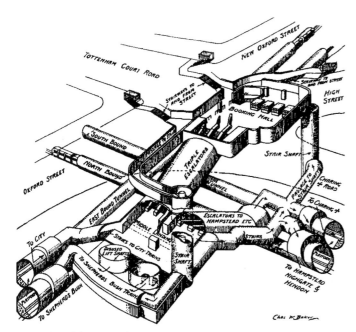

An overview of the proposed station reconstruction at Tottenham Court Road. This was a complex job at the time and required careful phasing. The original lifts from the Hampstead ticket hall dropped down from the right hand side of the ticket hall to the passage marked 'to Stair Shaft'.

When first opened most stations were also equipped with a 20,000 cubic feet per minute ventilation fan; air was drawn into the station by these fans and pumped down to the lower level via a circular duct that ran down the centre of the stairshaft to outlets on or under the platforms, warm air returning via the lift and stair shafts. This failed to deal with heat build up caused by improving train services and during the 1920s and 30s a huge amount of new ventilating plant was installed, often in vacated lift shafts.

GOLDERS GREEN DEPOT

The other major construction on the original Railway was the depot at Golders Green built (like the station) by Bott & Stennett and comprising 15 under-cover roads arranged within four sheds, five other roads and two traffic sidings. The capacity somewhat exceeded the number of cars owned by the line (many of which were outstabled at night at Highgate and Charing Cross) and for some years the depot was home to surplus Piccadilly Line cars as their depot was rather compact. With no connection with any other railway all maintenance and overhaul had to be done on the line and extensive facilities were available. Adjacent to the car sheds on the south side were the stores and offices, the latter comprising the general office, manager's office and timekeeper's office. On the next level was a very large drawing office. To keep track of the cars was a novel 'plug' board which graphically represented the layout of the roads with one plug position for each car's length of track. Numbered plugs (representing the car numbers) were inserted and moved around to represent the disposition of the stock at any time; this contrivance appears to have resulted from workmen in older depots losing time as they wandered around looking for the cars they had to work on. Also on the ground floor was a huge well-appointed machine shop with all the equipment required to service or repair just about anything; there were also specialist areas to deal with activities like refurbishing motors and very quickly this also took on the job of dealing with Piccadilly and Bakerloo traction motors. Most machine tools were powered by belts from overhead drive-shafts operated by BT-H electric motors. A wood workshop was also necessary and an area was set aside for repainting cars which in those days was done at least every two years—this seems to have been closed down on 7th January 1918 with functions transferred to the District's works & buildings workshops at Lillie Bridge, later re-established at Parson's Green.

In 1921 the Underground opened a central overhaul works at Acton. This took over a little of the load from Golders Green, but physical access with other lines was not possible until 27th March 1927 when a link with the Piccadilly opened at King's Cross. From 1924 Golders Green had also become the main depot for the reconstructed C&SLR and was now extremely busy and congested. At about this time a traverser was installed outside the car sheds at the north end so that individual cars could be moved from one road to another without shunting through the congested yard; this probably didn't have a long life and certainly didn't outlast the 1950s—the tracks are still there. Once the Piccadilly connection had opened and all heavy overhaul had been transferred to Acton the nature of the work undertaken at Golders Green was drastically simplified to deal with purely routine items, though with an ever increasing fleet size. It wasn't until the 1990s that it became feasible for depots such as Golders Green to return to more comprehensive overhaul of stock once the modern technology had made it possible. A useful feature at the depot was the avoidance of conductor rails inside the car sheds. To enable cars to be moved, overhead power lines were provided on which a trolley with power leads was mounted. A plug on the end of the leads could be inserted in a corresponding socket on any motor car to enable it to be moved, the trolley being pulled along at the same time; it was of course vital to remove the lead before the car concerned tried to leave the shed, a matter not always attended to, with inconvenient consequences. An automatic car washing plant came into service from early 1928, together with an additional 4-road shed bay. Eventually the entire available yard area was strewn with sidings, many hopelessly unable to accommodate full length trains but useful for storing uncoupled portions or odd cars. This inefficient and unexpandable layout was one of the reasons for the proposed Aldenham extension in the late 1930s which would have seen a vast new depot north of Elstree, but in the end Golders Green still copes.

STATIONS BRENT TO EDGWARE

The stations on the Hendon and Edgware extension were built to a quite different style, designed by Stanley Heaps, the Underground's architect. Each station with one exception was of portland stone construction and of commodious dimensions with wooden ticket booths known as 'passimeters'. There were bridge connections (subway at Brent, renamed Brent Cross in 1976) to the island platforms. Burnt Oak station was in so remote an area an

entirely new 320 ft access road was needed and a temporary booking hut was all that was provided (but the station still opened late, on 27th October 1924, owing to a building strike). The construction of the London County Council's Watling estate nearby threatened to generate traffic and a permanent building was completed in August 1928; the station didn't open on Sundays until 27th March 1927. At Hendon Central an auxiliary exit at the south end led directly into Queens Road and was an invaluable short cut for ticket-holders. Colindale received a somewhat similar exit in June 1927 to relieve the congestion in the ticket hall when vast crowds flocked to the flying displays at Hendon aerodrome, a huge source of occasional traffic on the new branch. Both these exits have been disused for at least a quarter century, the loss of the facility at Hendon being particularly irksome to those who had become accustomed to using it.

At Edgware, furious housing development caused traffic levels to increase rapidly, in turn requiring a better train service which required a new platform and more stabling accommodation. From 20th November 1932 a third platform was added on the west side of the existing station and an overall roof was provided, attached to the existing structure along its western edge. The new platform became Platform 1, the existing platforms and siding roads being renumbered one number higher during October. South of the station five new sidings (12-16) were laid to the west of the northbound line, but accessible only from Platform 1. A new crossover was laid to the south of the existing layout so trains from the new platform could return southbound, but they had no access to the shunting neck for the original sidings, which was far from ideal. Edgware also developed as an important transport interchange with many people continuing their journeys by the various bus routes that enjoyed use of the forecourt.

In the period 1935-40 a programme of new works was devised to extend the line beyond Edgware to Elstree and Aldenham. As part of the scheme a connection was also to be made to the old GNR line from Highgate and Finsbury Park which crossed the Hampstead Line just south of Edgware (the line was to be electrified to carry tube trains from either Finsbury Park or Archway); these works made it necessary to expand Edgware

The imposing new station building at Edgware was in Italianate style and incorporated a forecourt to accommodate the feeder buses. The road is yet to be made up and hedges are just visible in the foreground. Though vastly busier today, only the small section in the very centre now remains.

station enormously. Though these particular extensions did not finally come about, a great deal of demolition and rearrangement took place around the station and its approaches which faltered when war broke out in 1939. The station cutting was widened (again), Platform 1 lost its seven year old roof in anticipation of widening to accommodate another face on the west side, and sidings 12-15 were torn up (leaving No 16 on its own). On the east side, sidings 8-11 were reconstructed double length and twin shunting necks provided on an entirely new alignment that snuggled into the base of the GNR embankment. Some new but uncommissioned running lines were temporarily converted into sidings 17 and 18 and used for stock storage until disconnected and lifted in the late 1950s. A brand new signal box was structurally finished but abandoned only partly equipped and the old signal box at the south end of Platforms 2 and 3 had to make do until 1965 when more modern equipment could be afforded (partly installed in the empty pre-war cabin); the old signalbox structure still remains to be viewed as the only one of the 1920s surviving. The roof over Platform 1 was never replaced, but new stairs and a mean brick shelter were finally installed during 1965.

This view of an earnestly conducted inspection of Edgware's station garden in 1938 not only shows the signal box but is also one of the rare images of the roof over recently-added Platform 1, on the extreme left. The following year the new roof had gone and the cutting trimmed back to a new retaining wall. Most of the 1924 roof remains today.

PART THREE
THE TRAINS AND THE TRAIN SERVICES

The trains first used on the Hampstead Railway were built by the American Car & Foundry Company, and were assembled at Trafford Park in Manchester. The cars (an American term) were similar to those used on the Bakerloo but had a larger equipment compartment. The Bakerloo cars were also from AC&F and had been shipped over from the USA in 'knocked down' form but while the Hampstead cars do seem to have had American parts they also contained many British components and the equipment was made by BT-H in Rugby to American GEC design. The cars had gated end platforms via which passengers boarded and alighted; the platforms gave access to the car interiors via sliding end doors. Gatemen were stationed, one to each adjacent pair of platforms, to open and close the gates on adjacent cars. The motor cars had an enclosed cab for the driver, and the equipment compartment was situated immediately behind.

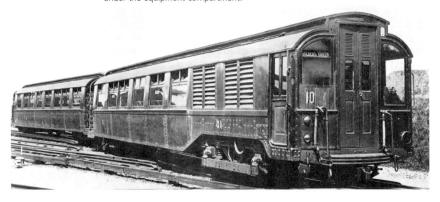

A motor car of 1907 origin showing the large motor bogie at the driving cab end, under the equipment compartment.

The 1902 agreement between the UERL and the CCE&HR provided for only 25 motor cars and 75 trailers, and while it is stated trains were to have been of five cars the proposed train make up is unknown—it is very difficult to see how this combination of cars could have made up 20 5-car trains. The cars were required to be built equal in quality 'to the carriages put on the New York Elevated Railway in 1892 and shall afford seating for 48 passengers'; they had to be capable of operating at an average speed of 14mph, including stops.

Once construction started the decision was made to intensify the service and the number of cars was increased to 150. The Hampstead stock as delivered comprised 60 motor cars and 90 trailers, enough to generate 30 5-car trains. Of the trailers 50 were fitted with driving controls on one of the gangways so that short trains could be operated with only one motor car. Driving from this position without the benefit of an enclosed cab was a somewhat draughty and dusty experience, even though a windscreen was fitted. This type of car became known as a control trailer and additional cars were converted later.

The cars were constructed of steel plates and girders and were about 50ft long and just 9ft 4ins high above rail level (6ft 4ins high internally). Motor cars seated 46 and trailers 52 passengers (on average just exceeding contractual requirement). Wooden fittings were employed internally, all wood being mahogany, specially treated to be fireproof. The motor cars were each fitted with two 200hp motors, controlled by electrical equipment mounted on the same car; this was operated on the multiple unit system (perfected in America) from a controller on the leading car. Acceleration was not automatic and drivers (termed motormen) had to use judgement in operating the equipment as an attempt to accelerate too quickly would spin the motor wheels or cause the equipment to disengage on overload. Braking was achieved by the use of the Westinghouse quick-acting air brake with its built-in safety features; cast iron brake blocks were dispensed with in favour of Frood's patent blocks comprising a mixture of canvas and pitch in an attempt to reduce the amount of metallic dust that tended to interfere with the signalling (more traditional cast iron blocks were introduced later and the metallic dust had the

A 'gate stock' train at Highgate in 1907. This view shows the arc light (above the train) and incandescent lights along the wall. The signalbox is at the far end of the platform. Water spillage seems to emanate from the fire hydrant cabinet next to the signalbox. (There is another version of this image where someone has gone to a lot of trouble to retouch the platform to hide the water.)

predictable outcome of generating 'smoulderings' and signal failures until more satisfactory non metallic blocks emerged just before the Second World War). Train lighting emanated from sets of incandescent lamps mounted in the ceiling, several lamps being electrically connected in series with each other to handle the traction supply from which they (and all other train equipment) were fed. They were probably of the unsatisfactory carbon filament

type and in February 1908 two trains had been designated to test a new type of lamp, the lamp holders being painted silver to remind staff that only special lamps should be used.

Trains carried headlamps with a colour code to indicate destination: Charing Cross and Golders Green required one white and one green lamp to be shown, Highgate required two white lights and Hampstead two green lights. From the passenger's point of view a more obvious means was called for to identify to which branch a train was destined, and it was felt helpful to provide signs in the front window announcing each train's destination. The signs were double sided enamelled iron plates capable of showing Charing Cross, Hampstead, Highgate or Golders Green, as required—there were in those days no train indicators on any of the platforms, though staff were encouraged to bawl out essential information. Signs on the front were evidently found quite insufficient and from May 1908 additional signs were made available on the sides of each car. It was not until Summer 1926 that indicators began to be installed on the platforms to prophesy where the first two or three trains might be heading. Charing Cross, Leicester Square, Tottenham Court Road and Euston were the first to be fitted and could display the next three trains; most other stations followed later though many only showed two trains.

In addition to the Hampstead's own stock, some cars were available from the Bakerloo and Piccadilly Lines where traffic was slow to develop and many cars were spare. A few of these ended up at Golders Green and went into service, and in due course these extra cars became a permanent feature.

The first trains operated on an experimental basis from 13th May 1907 when two empty 3-car trains were put into operation for testing, maintaining a 30-minute service on each branch; the service reversed south to north at Mornington Crescent as the line farther south was not sufficiently advanced, and the train on the Golders Green branch reversed at Hampstead for similar reasons.

Public services began on 22nd June. The railway press suggests the initial train services on each branch operated at 4-minute intervals, combining into two minutes south of Camden Town, but only one in three trains ran north of Hampstead to Golders Green, which had a 12-minute service. It was stated that frequencies were slightly reduced outside peak times (probably to 3-minutes).

Train services varied considerably over the next decade and the make up of trains was also subject to constant adjustment. For some years it was not felt necessary to adopt formal timetables and trains were run to a rigorous set of station-to-station headways and running times (to the nearest five seconds); until the First World War 15 seconds was defined as the standard station 'dwell' time,

and time to reverse at the terminals could be as short as a minute—though the large train staff helped manage this pace. In September 1907 the running times were accelerated in the light of experience, Charing Cross to Golders Green being $20^1/2$ minutes northbound and $18^1/2$ minutes southbound. In the early days traffic on the Highgate branch was heavier than on the Hampstead, but traffic overall was very slow to build up and was many years before even 100 of the line's 150 cars were needed for service. The September 1907 services were reduced to 6-minutes on each branch (still 12 minutes to Golders Green), using 10 x 4-car trains on the Highgate service and 11 x 3-car services on the Hampstead branch. All trains were 2-car off peak (the Highgate trains were uncoupled while the Hampstead trains were changed over for shorter ones at Golders Green).

Over the following few years a wide range of different train make ups was deployed to accurately match traffic levels, which quite slowly but reassuringly responded. In December 1907 train service departure times were standardized at the termini, based on trains leaving Golders Green on the hour then every ten minutes; intervals remained static for a while but clockface operation disappeared when service levels were increased the following year. From February 1908 the Hampstead branch was using 4-car trains in the peaks, with a combination of 5- and 6-car trains on the Highgate branch (requiring a total of 80 cars).

In May 1908 running times were further reduced, Golders Green to Charing Cross being now $16^1/2$ minutes northbound and 16 minutes southbound, but in subsequent years they increased as traffic grew. At the same time an attempt was made to run a slightly more intense service to Highgate in the morning peak (only) with corresponding shortening of trains to 4-cars (except for two 6-car trains), but this asymmetric service would have been awkward to operate and in later schedules intervals on each branch were equalized again. In July 1908 a special train was operated on weekdays. Leaving Highgate at 7.59am it ran non stop to Camden Town where it picked up again; a second train operated in the same fashion from 5th October, leaving Highgate at 8.39am. From November 1908 intervals on each branch were reduced to $3^1/2$ minutes giving a combined service south of Camden Town of $1^3/4$

minutes, but trains were correspondingly shortened and even with three 6-car trains helping out on the Highgate branch there were just 72 cars in service. From 30th September 1909 things got more interesting with the a basic service of 20 trains an hour on each branch of assorted 3-, 4- and 5-car sets on the Highgate branch and 3-car on the Hampstead branch. In addition there were now four peak-hour trains that ran non-stop between Golders Green and Euston (or vice versa) which gave a combined service south of Camden Town of 42 trains an hour, only achievable by keeping the station dwell times low. This still used just two thirds of the rolling stock that had been purchased.

Headway clocks had been installed on 26th August 1907 at Mornington Crescent (southbound) and both northbound platforms at Camden Town. These started at zero and automatically counted the minutes since the previous train; motormen were trained to try and keep to the scheduled headway and the clocks were there to give them guidance. Staff were warned that to follow the previous southbound train at a shorter headway than 1 1/4 minutes would cause it to be checked outside Tottenham Court Road, and that passengers did not like being detained in a tunnel.

The Hampstead Railway's management constantly fiddled with the non-stopping arrangements and the times of first and last trains, especially the latter. In September 1909 first trains left the termini around 5.20am and ran until about 1am (12.45am in the case of the Golders Green branch); when the line opened first trains had been about 20 minutes later and last trains 20-30 minutes earlier. In those days evening theatre traffic was heavy and needed especially close attention. For example in November 1908 two 6-car trains were put into service on Wednesdays and Thursdays only, timed to leave Charing Cross at 11.17 and 11.27pm, each serving Highgate. From October 1910 the remaining Hampstead reversers were all extended to Golders Green, providing that station with some 300 trains a day. In addition some special theatre trains were laid on in each direction that non-stopped several stations, the journey between Golders Green and Leicester Square being accomplished at an average speed of 23.72mph in just 14 minutes (normal time was nearer 20); the forward train left Golders Green

at 7.16pm non-stopping Belsize Park to Goodge Street and the return working left Charing Cross at 11.15pm. While a similar service also served Highgate three years later it is difficult to imagine people actually waiting specifically for the forward trains as they could hardly overtake the usual service trains, one reason they did not perhaps endure.

When services were extended to Charing Cross (Embankment) all trains operated around the loop and this avoided the time wasted in crews walking from one end of the train to the other. Loop working was not without disadvantages though. Cars were cabled and piped so that the relevant hose and jumper connections between them were directly opposite each other and the introduction of a reversing loop meant that cars frequently got turned around; this meant 'turned' cars could not couple to 'unturned' cars and with all the short and different length trains in use this was inconvenient and could give rise to embarrassing delays, especially if the service got disrupted. In practice it meant more spare cars were needed to cover for the slight loss of flexibility—not a problem in the early days when there was plenty of spare stock but it became an irritating characteristic of the Hampstead Line and the Northern in later years. To help alleviate the turning problem a turntable was installed at the back of Golders Green yard so that cars intended for maintenance would enter the shops the correct way round.

During the First World War traffic levels on all of the tubes increased dramatically and the Hampstead Line emerged operating in the peaks some 38 trains an hour in 5-car formations with twelve 3-car trains off peak. By this time the LER had found that running more trains than 38 per hour was no longer possible owing to increasing boarding times. To meet demand it was now necessary to embark on train lengthening and this required substantially more cars than the Hampstead owned. A range of similar cars borrowed from the Bakerloo and Piccadilly Lines were pressed into service (a few had never been in service before) and the number of control trailers had to be increased by fitting driving equipment to regular trailers.

The 1920 train service peaked at 37 trains an hour and required 26 trains, eight stabling at Highgate and the remainder stabling at Golders Green; four trains now operated as 6-car sets. The non-stopping arrangements had now settled down and operated mainly in the peaks. Northbound non-stopping patterns not only differed from southbound, but also differed from one peak to the other, which must have made communicating this to passengers a challenge. There is a theme, which relied on each successive set of four trains using each non-stop pattern in turn, half the service missing out Mornington Crescent, another station to its south and a station on either branch; Camden Town could only be missed northbound as southbound trains were likely to be checked anyway.

STATIONS NON-STOPPED

Southbound Morning and Evening FROM Golders Green
Alternate 1: Chalk Farm

Alternate 2: Belsize Park and Mornington Crescent

Southbound Morning and Evening FROM Highgate
Alternate 1: South Kentish Town

Alternate 2: Mornington Crescent

Northbound Morning TO Golders Green
Alternate 1: Goodge Street and Mornington Crescent

Alternate 2: Warren Street, Chalk Farm and Belsize Park

Northbound Morning TO Highgate
Alternate 1: Warren Street, South Kentish Town and Tufnell Park

Alternate 2: Goodge Street, Mornington Crescent and Kentish Tn

Northbound Evening TO Golders Green
Alternate 1: Goodge Street

Alternate 2: Warren Street, Mornington Crescent and Camden Tn

Northbound Evening TO Highgate
Alternate 1: Goodge Street and South Kentish Town

Alternate 2: Mornington Crescent and Tufnell Park

It will be noted that the longer pre-First World War non-stop runs from Golders Green (described earlier) had now gone: they would have been inoperable under these dense service conditions. The special theatre trains had been abandoned during the war but were resurrected by 1920, now only running in the northbound direction and leaving Charing Cross at 11.6pm and 11.30pm for Golders Green, and 11.27 for Highgate (timings were slightly different on Saturdays). These trains stopped only at Charing Cross, Strand, Leicester Square, Hampstead (where applicable) and their final destination; Golders Green was reached 16 minutes after leaving Charing Cross (standard running time being 21 minutes). In addition the Highgate and Golders Green services now interworked so a train from one branch would usually return to the other. This facilitated uncoupling between the Monday-Friday peaks when 21 successive trains at 4-minute intervals each uncoupled two (or three) cars. Some of these lay over in the short sidings north of the platforms while others had to scuttle into the depot without impeding the next incoming train. Trains did not then uncouple in the evenings or on Saturdays, but ran as 3-car sets on Sundays until coupling up from about 2pm. The price paid for an interworked service is that when delays occurred it was impossible to confine the resulting disruption merely to one branch.

The 1921 industrial unrest caused services to close down an hour earlier from 1st August but this was thought to inconvenience (in particular) the fraternity of restaurant waiters who couldn't get home and from 7th November special late trains were put on each of the LER Lines. The Hampstead Line trains came into service from Strand and the Golders Green train departed at 12.49am and called at Leicester Square, Tottenham Court Road, Camden Town and then all stations; the Highgate train departed two minutes earlier with a similar stopping pattern to Camden Town then stopping only at Kentish Town and Highgate. It seems they were not well patronised and were withdrawn from 16th January 1922.

The opening of the Edgware extension offered new opportunities to introduce complexity. Traffic was initially so sparse that until 12th June 1927 through services were not operated on Sundays and a shuttle train rattled up and down between Edgware and Golders Green, turning in the middle road and connecting into Charing Cross trains reversing in the outer platforms. Burnt Oak station was in any case not opened on Sundays until 27th March 1927. When the Edgware extension opened it wasn't clear how traffic would develop and both City and Charing Cross services ran through. Experience soon showed that the existing inhabitants showed little inclination to travel to the City so from 4th May 1925 trains via Bank were largely cut back to Golders Green and more Charing Cross trains sent through, City passengers making a convenient cross platform change at Golders Green. From 28th September 1925 alternate trains from Edgware in the morning peaks ran non stop to Hendon, taking advantage of the thin service north of Colindale to get up speed without catching up the train in front. As traffic built up this pattern soon became unworkable and all trains called at all stations.

The coupling with the C&SLR made service operation so complex that the more general form of non-stopping became a serious irritation for little benefit; except for the specific trains or services just referred to the complicated non-stopping arrangements were greatly simplified from 28th September 1925. Thenceforth all Edgware branch trains forthwith missed out Mornington Crescent in either direction, an oddity that continued until as late as 17th October 1966. In addition, until the Second World War, some northbound peak hour Edgware branch trains also missed out Camden Town.

Passive provision had been made at Brent for passing loops to allow non-stops to overtake trains that called there. From 13th June 1927 use was first made of these when the 8.58am departure from Edgware was arranged to run fast to Golders Green, overtaking the train in front (ex Colindale) at Brent; this train also non-stopped Mornington Crescent and Warren Street and was booked to reach Charing Cross at 9.28; there was no return working. From 30th January 1928 a second non-stop train began operating from Edgware at 8.19am, also overtaking the previous train at Brent and resuming normal operation from Golders Green; this time the train ran through to the City with an equivalent

Front cover of a Hampstead Line working timetable of 1920. Unlike today's timetables only the bare minimum of timing points were shown.

return starting from Tooting at 5.12pm, running via Bank (departing 5.39pm). This was hardly extensive use of the infrastructure provided at Brent and when the service finished in July 1936 it was little missed. The Underground's signal engineer was quite rude about the operating manager's dedication to this form of working and thought 'it was a complete accident' if even a minute were saved in practice.

After 1920 the proportion of 6-car trains gradually increased (uncoupling into two 3-car portions) and became standard by the mid 1920s with some 7-car trains entering service too. Once the C&SLR connections had opened at Camden Town and Kennington the train services were quite interesting. At first each branch received an equal service from Charing Cross or the C&SLR. The November 1928 schedule saw the Charing Cross route served by 28 trains an hour in each peak, splitting at Camden Town almost equally into Highgate or Golders Green services (which thinned out either there or Colindale). Beyond Colindale, services in the busiest hour increased from 13 to 15 7-car trains compared with the 1926 timetable. Meanwhile the new City services operating north of Colindale doubled from four to eight 6-car trains. 36 trains an hour operated south of Kennington, a dramatic increase since opening in 1926. Until the Second World War all southbound evening peak hour trains destined for Morden (via Charing Cross) non-stopped Kennington. This schedule required 94 trains in peak service, or 603 cars in all. A further 46 cars were injected into the line for the 1929 schedule, with a further 36 anticipated. From about 1932 all trains were normally of 7-cars length and this endured until the introduction of the present 1996 stock.

As services continued to develop it became obvious that not only did the Edgware and Highgate branches require unequal services as Edgware traffic developed, so too did the Charing Cross and City routes. The Summer 1937 timetable, for example, shows a 2½–3-minute service operating to the City, with a slight bias towards trains from Edgware, while a 1½-minute service operated

A motor car of 1923 origin showing the centre air-worked doors and the considerably cleaner lines compared with the original cars. From 1926 the front end of new cars were further tidied up, with older cars soon modified to match. Trailers had two sets of air doors on each side.

via Charing Cross equally from Edgware/Colindale and Highgate but with the odd 'push in' train starting at Golders Green which again increased frequencies on that branch. This kind of asymmetric operation was not the easiest to operate. This timetable, incidentally, required 95 trains (665 cars) across the whole of the Morden-Edgware Line in the peak, all of 7-cars (the winter services were even more intense and required 99 trains). Outside busy hours trains now uncoupled into 3-car and 4-car sets, the former used on the Highgate branch and Golders Green via City service, and the latter on the Edgware-Kennington via Charing Cross service. Until this happy arrangement was found to be the most satisfactory to operate, earlier attempts to deploy 7-car operation had seen a variety of train formations, including sets that uncoupled into 2-car and 5-car portions off-peak. The theatre trains do not seem to have survived the interconnection with the C&SLR but the traffic problem seems to have been addressed by coupling up the service to 7-cars again for the last hour of traffic.

As may be inferred from what has just been said, the rapid extension and development of the Hampstead Line during the 1920s required much additional rolling stock; the existing design of 'gate stock' was quite unsuitable for further development and required trains of entirely new thinking. With that object in mind six sample cars were ordered from different manufacturers and tested on the Piccadilly Line between a pair of gate stock motor cars modernized by fitting air-operated doors in the centre of the

carbody. Once service experience and passenger views had been assessed this train was transferred to the Hampstead Line in August 1923, in time for the opening to Hendon. At about the same time orders were placed for a new fleet of trains to service the

A short train approaches Edgware in 1927, control trailer leading. Trees testify to the slightly slow building development.

Edgware extension and C&SLR reopening. These comprised 191 cars intended to operate in 5-car sets (uncoupling into 2-car and 3-car portions) and were sufficient for about 33 trains plus spares. In 1924 127 additional cars were ordered to service C&SLR reopening to Clapham Common and lengthening the fleet from 5-car to 6-car trains while in 1925 a further 120 cars were ordered for service augmentation and further train lengthening. Of this new fleet 330 (including the sample cars) were technically owned by the LER and 114 by the C&SLR although they were operated as a single fleet. The cars were built by Cammell-Laird (155 cars), Metropolitan Carriage, Wagon & Finance Co (200 cars) and the Birmingham Railway Carriage & Wagon Co (86 cars). The new design comprised entirely enclosed vehicles. Motor cars had a single pair of air-operated doors towards the centre of the cars and a hinged door for the guard's use at the trailing end whilst trailers and control trailers had two symmetrically disposed pairs of air-operated doors per car side, the control trailer having a driving cab at one end. Altogether the fleet comprised 181 motor cars, 128 control trailers and 135 trailers (444 cars in all), enough for roundly 64 trains plus spare cars. The balance of the train service was provided by the remaining gate stock trains, though as far as possible they were confined to duties entirely in tunnel.

The introduction of new trains not only made the gate stock look old fashioned but also demonstrated how slow boarding and alighting was, encouraging the view that the obsolete design should be replaced, though the cars were only 20 years old. To facilitate this, 112 additional cars were ordered in 1926 and 170 in 1927, all by Metro Cammell, comprising 127 motor cars and 155 trailers. The increased fleet size allowed for gradual train lengthening to 7-cars as well as gate stock replacement and with the sample cars provided sufficient stock for a 91-train service. No new control trailers were needed as the 7-car trains ran in formations either M-T-CT+M-T-T-M or M-T-T-M+CT-T-M, trains uncoupling off peak (where the '+' sign is shown). The last gate stock train on the Hampstead Line ran on 31st January 1929, and subsequent builds of new stock for other lines and transfers of cars between lines further increased the fleet size so by the mid 1930s it could to provide for a 99-train winter service of all 7-car trains.

PART FOUR
THE SIGNALLING AND TRACK

When the District was electrified the Americans were keen to use the latest technology to improve the volume of trains it was possible to operate while keeping costs low. They decided to adapt the system used on the Boston Elevated Railroad and, leaving nothing to chance, converted a built but unopened section of the District between Ealing and South Harrow for 4-rail electric operation with automatic signalling. Opened in 1903 and judged a complete success a similar signalling system was adopted for the main part of the District and the three new tubes.

Following these experiments the traction supply on all Yerkes lines was delivered by an 'insulated return' system comprising two conductor rails, the centre negative and the outer rail (18 inches outside one or other running rail) was positive, being respectively $1\frac{1}{2}$ and 3 inches higher than the running rails so the trains' pick up shoes could clear the running rails at pointwork. This type of electrification simplified the intended automatic signalling and was familiar to the Americans. British-made conductor rails rested in rectangular porcelain insulators and insulated anchors were installed periodically to discourage movement—current rails on earlier railways had tended to 'creep' by constant sweeping with collector shoes. The track itself was laid in 45ft lengths with rails imported America, though the hard wearing pointwork was of British origin. Sleepers were of Australian Karri wood with their ends embedded in concrete and centre resting on crushed granite.

The essence of the new signalling was completely automatic operation where possible. Whether or not a signal showed 'danger' or 'clear' was determined entirely by the presence, or not, of a train ahead. Instead of lots of signalmen regulating the train movements they were picked up automatically by electrical track circuits which detected the presence of train wheels on any given section of track (track circuits were by no means new, but had not previously been used for unsupervised train control). Track circuits were created by dividing the rails into sections up to 700ft long by means of insulated joints and applying a voltage between the two rails at one end. An electrical 'relay' device at the other end

An example of a tunnel signal installed on the Charing Cross loop. The weighted spectacle glasses are raised and lowered in front of the lamp housing to show the appropriate aspect; the air motor and control valves are situated behind. At track level a trainstop is visible, trip arm raised. The twin tunnel telephone wires are just visible higher up the right hand tunnel wall.

detected this voltage and controlled contacts that caused the signal to show 'clear'. As soon as a train moved onto the track circuit the wheels would short circuit the relay depriving it of current and releasing the contacts through which the signal circuit operated, putting it to danger. By placing signals a suitable distance ahead of their controlling track circuits they would return to danger shortly after the rear carriage had passed, and remain at danger until the rear of the train was safely beyond the signal ahead—there would **always** be at least one danger signal behind a train. This type of signalling was called fully automatic signalling, and signals so controlled received the number of the track circuit preceded by the letter 'S'.

Where junctions or crossovers existed it was still necessary to have a signalman to switch routes, but signals and points were power operated. In conjunction with the Westinghouse Brake Company a miniature lever frame had been developed which still used the completely trusted system of mechanically interlocked levers to prevent conflicting routes being set up and to hold routes actually being traversed. However instead of the cumbersome wires and rodding used in older signal cabins the levers actuated electrical circuits to switch points and operate signals by means of compressed air. Signal control circuits were overlaid on the track circuits so signals could not be cleared unless the correct route was set up and the road was clear—they would return to danger

This plan shows the track layout and signalling arrangements on the Hampstead Railway at opening and uses standard signal diagram symbols.

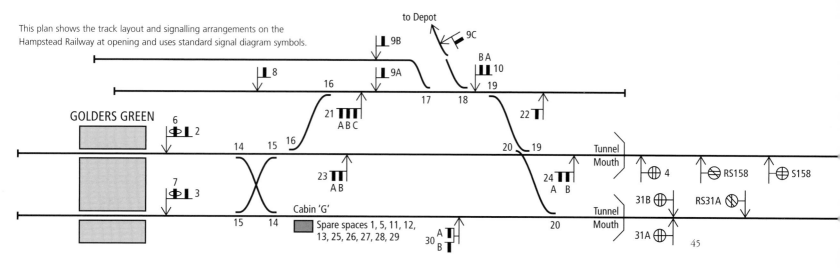

GOLDERS GREEN

Cabin 'G'

Spare spaces 1, 5, 11, 12, 13, 25, 26, 27, 28, 29

automatically after passage of each train. The signal frames were arranged such that operation of approach track circuits, or those reading over pointwork, would lock the relevant signal lever in its reverse position, effectively locking the route until each train movement had been safely completed. Since signalmen could not necessarily see the trains their position had to be indicated some other way. At Golders Green, Highgate and Charing Cross the signal cabin track diagrams were back-illuminated so that each track circuit glowed when clear, but showed as a dark strip when occupied by a train. At Hampstead and Mornington Crescent (which were not intended to be permanently manned) separate track circuit indications were shown comprising solenoid operating flags (or banners) which showed in triangular shaped windows on a painted track diagram—these cabins could also be left unattended by leaving the signal levers for the through routes reversed in the frame, at other cabins signal levers had to be operated afresh for each train. This type of signalling was initially called Interlocking Signalling, but quite quickly became known as 'Semi-Automatic' and signals received the number of the controlling lever preceded by a code letter specific to the signal cabin; the letters were 'C' for Charing Cross (11-lever frame), 'D' for Mornington Crescent (11-lever frame), 'E' for Camden Town (7-lever frame), 'F' for Hampstead (11-lever frame), 'G' for Golders Green (31-lever frame) and 'H' for Highgate (15-lever frame).

At Golders Green, in the open air, the signals were of the air-operated lower quadrant semaphore type, including ground level shunting signals, as on the District. Since there was not room for these in tunnels, air-operated moving spectacles were employed; these moved in front of an oil lamp and thus showed an appropriate coloured light to an approaching driver. The natural position of the spectacle was in its lower position, presenting a red aspect. When

The signal box at Mornington Crescent controlled the emergency crossover there. The box and its fittings were typical of most Hampstead Railway signal boxes. The track diagram is equipped with solenoid-operated indicators to show which track circuits are occupied by trains.

the track ahead was clear, an air motor pushed the spectacle upwards to show a green aspect; any failure of electricity or air or any track circuit failure would result in the spectacle falling to the lower (danger) position. Oil lamps did not prove very satisfactory: they had the advantage that if signalling current did fail for some reason then a driver would still see a red light. However the lamps became sooty, or blew out completely, and drivers were eventually warned (perhaps with a touch of optimism) to watch out for signals showing no light and work out whether to carry on or not depending on the position of the spectacle. Within a year or so the

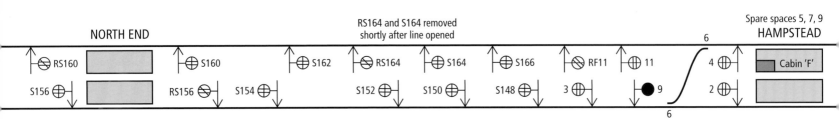

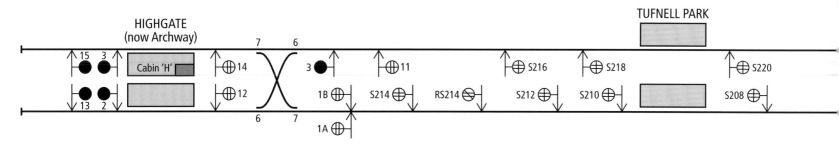

oil lamps were replaced by electric lamps in the same housings. The initial installation on the Hampstead comprised 60 working levers, 131 track circuits, 80 automatic signals with 17 repeaters and 53 semi-automatic signals with 3 repeaters.

Again following American practice it was felt that with so many signals and such an intensive service and with limited visibility motormen could not be relied upon to stop correctly (or at all) at danger signals, the consequences being potentially catastrophic. To mitigate this danger automatic train stopping equipment was fitted from the start. These comprised a track-mounted air operated motor pushing against a spring; with no air applied the spring raised a small lever (the trainstop) just outside the right hand running rail but when the associated signal was clear the air motor pushed the lever down, out of the way. In the corresponding position at the front of each train was another lever (the tripcock) which was connected directly to the train line brake pipe on the train. If a train attempted to pass a signal at danger the tripcock would strike the trainstop and apply the emergency brake. Signalling was generally arranged so that any previous train would have to be beyond this emergency braking distance before the following train could approach the protecting signal, thus preserving an adequate margin of safety. In addition to standard 'stop' signals there were a small number of repeaters where visibility was restricted, usually by curvature; these used standard

The approach to Hendon Central shortly before opening shows a number of new coloured light signals about to be commissioned. In those days route indicators were unknown, and separate signals were provided for each route. The boxes lying alongside the track are electric trainstops awaiting installation. The rural feel is still evident.

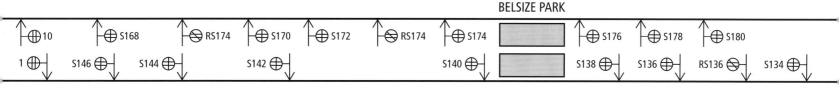

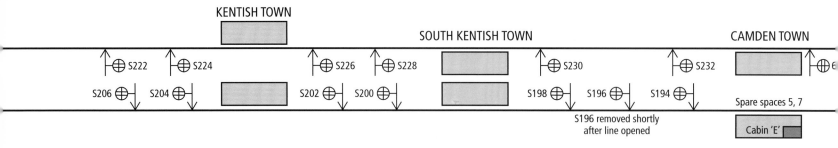

KENTISH TOWN — SOUTH KENTISH TOWN — CAMDEN TOWN

S222 · S224 · S226 · S228 · S230 · S232

S206 · S204 · S202 · S200 · S198 · S196 · S194

Spare spaces 5, 7

S196 removed shortly after line opened

Cabin 'E'

spectacles but with an orange instead of a red aspect, and no trainstop. Tripcocks operated in a punishing environment were checked daily in the depot. In December 1923 the static tests were reinforced by an automatic tester fitted on the southbound road at Strand. An approaching train illuminated a purple lamp fitted at the southern headwall and correct operation of the tester treadle by the tripcock would cancel the indicator; if it stayed alight it meant something was wrong and the train would have to be withdrawn from service for checking.

Installation of moving spectacle signals continued for long enough to be employed along the Charing Cross loop, but after the First World War most new tunnel signals were of a simple twin lamp lantern style with no moving parts, and by the time of the Second World War all the moving spectacle types had gone. Other improvements were made over time. The original track circuits used direct current circuits, but from the early 1920s new installations used alternating current, allowing a number of safety improvements to be made, and within the next twenty years all the signalling had been converted. More signals and track circuits were added in abundance, starting shortly after opening and continuing until the late 1930s. Stations originally had just one 'home' signal (the signal protecting the platform), but as traffic grew and station dwell times increased any following train would be held at the home causing a delay that rebounded. By adding first one, then

two (and occasionally more) additional signals between the home and the platform that cleared successively as the train got on the move, so following trains could often avoid an unnecessary stop or, if stopped, could get going almost immediately the delayed train started up. Busy Tottenham Court Road was one of the first stations to benefit from additional home signals. Other technical improvements made during the 1930s included rearranged wiring so signals went to danger as soon as they were passed, so obviating any possibility a green light might ever be showing behind a train (particularly a short train), and 'trainstop proving' where to reduce risk further a trainstop was proved to have returned to the operative position—if it hadn't then the previous signal and trainstop were held at danger.

When the Hendon and Edgware extensions opened the Underground decided to deploy all-electric apparatus and no air supply was provided. Signals were of the then-quite-innovative long-range coloured light type, said to be visible from at least 1000 yards even in poor conditions, and trainstops and point mechanisms were electrically operated. Signal cabins were provided at Brent (cabin AA, 11-levers, initially out of use), Hendon (AB, 11 levers), Colindale (AC, 15-levers) and Edgware (AE, 23-levers). As already mentioned, at Brent provision had been made for passing loops to be installed which were commissioned on 3rd January 1925, though not normally used until 1927. The

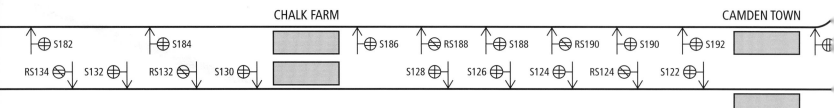

CHALK FARM — CAMDEN TOWN

S182 · S184 · S186 · RS188 · S188 · RS190 · S190 · S192

RS134 · S132 · RS132 · S130 · S128 · S126 · S124 · RS124 · S122

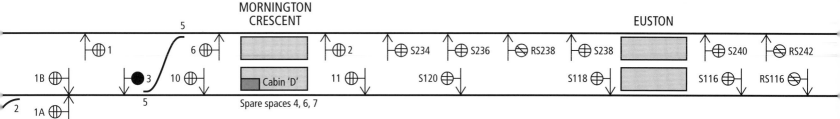

MORNINGTON CRESCENT 5   EUSTON

⊕ 1   6 ⊕   ⊕ 2   ⊕ S234   ⊕ S236   ⊗ RS238   ⊕ S238   ⊕ S240   ⊗ RS242

1B ⊕   ● 3   10 ⊕   Cabin 'D'   11 ⊕   S120 ⊕   S118 ⊕   S116 ⊕   RS116 ⊗

2   1A ⊕   5   Spare spaces 4, 6, 7

use to which these loops were put could hardly have justified their expense and the fast trains last ran on 11th July 1936, the loops being decommissioned on the night of 22nd August when the cabin was permanently closed (the pointwork was taken out just a week later).

The cabin at Hendon at first controlled the two crossovers south of the station required when it was the temporary terminus; it was usually unmanned after the extension to Edgware opened when the facing crossover was removed, but finally closed at the end of 1930 (though the remaining trailing crossover had actually been removed on 16th June 1930). The cabin at Colindale was not the luckiest. The all-electric style 'K' Westinghouse frame did not incorporate so-called 'indication locking' of point levers, by means of which a point lever would otherwise be locked in mid stroke until each set of points was proved to have completed their throw (this was because electric point mechanisms operate quite slowly and there are other means of ensuring a route is properly set). One day in early August 1925 the signalmen failed to notice that after letting a train out of the siding and putting the levers back he got no 'normal' point indication. The outlet points on the crossover from the siding had failed to respond, though the trailing end by the cabin had thrown normally. He then set a route for another train to enter the siding (these did respond) but could not clear the controlling signal. At the same time the next southbound train from Edgware stopped at the home signal which also failed to clear owing to the failure. The signalmen failed to notice the crossover from the siding was showing no indication (which would immediately have shown what the trouble was). He assumed from the levers that the routes were correctly set and then made arrangements for both trains to proceed past their respective

danger signals; the northbound train entered the siding and ran through the faulty points breaking off one switch rail completely and badly buckling the other; this may be one reason why the Underground was disinclined to make further use of all electric equipment and returned to electro-pneumatic systems, though

This view of Hendon Central immediately before opening shows the new signal box at the north end of the platforms. Electrification was later extended into the tunnels which were used to stable service trains for a few weeks before the Edgware extension opened. The 'Central' part of the station name was usually given in brackets prior to November 1923, but permanent signage always showed Hendon Central.

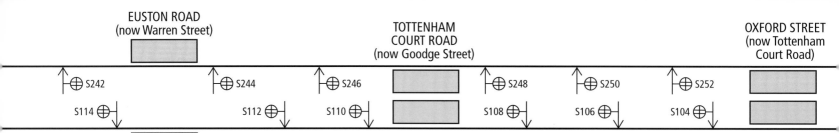

EUSTON ROAD
(now Warren Street)

TOTTENHAM
COURT ROAD
(now Goodge Street)

OXFORD STREET
(now Tottenham
Court Road)

S242   S244   S246   S248   S250   S252

S114   S112   S110   S108   S106   S104

retaining long range coloured light signal heads. Ten years later, on 4th August 1935, an aircraft associated with Hendon Aerodrome managed to land on the railway line near Colindale creating a violent short circuit that found its way into the signal cabin at the north end of the platform setting it on fire and causing complete destruction. Incredibly hard work by the engineers meant automatic through running was introduced within hours and a temporary replacement cabin was established by the 18th August on the flower beds by the southbound line, using an old signal frame commandeered from South Kensington signal school. A permanent new signal box was opened on the original site on 19th April 1936, this time of fireproof construction that set a new standard for the whole Underground. In the early 1950s the remaining all electric apparatus was finally removed in favour of conventional air operated equipment, except for the coloured light signals which of course had already set their own new standard.

To accommodate the extension to Edgware, Golders Green's simple layout became rather more complicated. The new layout had to accommodate through services whilst still retaining facilities for part of the service still to reverse and to go into and out of service. Works included adding a new platform face and track on the east side, another scissors crossover and two additional traffic sidings between the running lines south of the station (partly to deal with uncoupled cars stabled off-peak). Reworking the track layout took place over two years and required enlargement of the signal frame by adding a new 8-lever section at the north end. A new road was added at the south end of the depot so that signalled movements between the depot and the station could be separated from those merely shunting; there wasn't enough room for the upgraded reception road to accommodate a 7-car train so a third tunnel was drilled into the Hampstead ridge

In 1935 an RAF plane crashed on the line about 200 yards north of Colindale and the resulting short circuit set the signal box on fire and it was completely destroyed. It was not considered wholly unremarkable in those days that train services resumed within hours.

about 1½-cars long, partly occupied by an oil buffer stop. In May 1932 a 4-lever mechanical ground frame was installed in the shunters' cabin to enable the main crossovers at the depot entrance to be operated from under cover, these levers also operated special shunting signs (looking a bit like semaphore signals) which indicated when the routes into the shunting neck were available. In April 1925 further complication was endured by adding a northbound loop line next to the running line south of the station, mainly so that trains due to reverse there (but finding the middle road occupied) could slumber quietly out of the way awaiting a

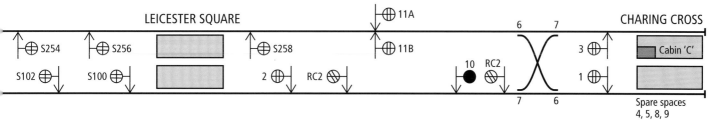

LEICESTER SQUARE   11A   6   7   CHARING CROSS

S254   S256   S258   11B   3   Cabin 'C'

S102   S100   2   RC2   10   RC2   1

7   6   Spare spaces
4, 5, 8, 9

This image graphically shows the frantic activity involved in one of the stagework alterations at Golders Green. There are well over a hundred people on site.

This view of Golders Green immediately after opening of the Hendon extension shows the new platform face on the extreme right, but little other change, and the original semaphores survive for the moment.

path without blocking the northbound line; installation of this road required widening the cutting on the west side, shifting the northbound line to the west and complex adjustments to the track on the approach to the station. The resited northbound line came into use on 12th April and the new loop on 26th April. After track rearrangement the signals at Golders Green were mostly of the modern coloured light pattern but two new 2-arm semaphores were installed as inner-homes on the northbound main and loop lines; despite being relocated more than once these lasted until October 1950 when signal indications in the area were upgraded to London Transport's latest standard.

When Edgware station was enlarged in 1931 the signalling needed rearranging and the signal frame enlarging by adding a new 12-lever section at the left hand end. Even before 1931 the original signalled capacity between Golders Green and Edgware was proving woefully inadequate and a number of additional signals were provided in 1928/9 to ensure capacity was at least equal to that south of Golders Green. Meanwhile the reconstruction of Camden Town junctions in 1924 had required entirely new signalling controlled from a new 43-lever frame in an enlarged signal box at the south end of the northbound Highgate branch platform. The new frame (like its predecessor coded 'E') was also arranged to control the layout at Mornington Crescent and the signal box there was closed.

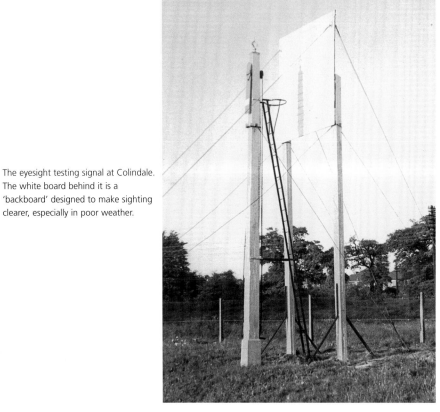

The eyesight testing signal at Colindale. The white board behind it is a 'backboard' designed to make sighting clearer, especially in poor weather.

Five stages of track layout at Golders Green. This sequence of diagrams on the facing page has Golders Green platforms to the north and the tunnel mouth to the south. It shows how in a period of two years the original configuration was transformed into something resembling that of today. The only interruption to service was over one holiday weekend. Today's layout differs only that the scissors crossover on the southbound side has given way to an additional crossover from the middle road.

The bold lines depict new construction, relative to the previous diagram; thin grey lines show what has been removed.

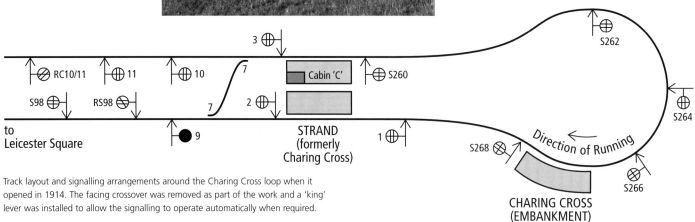

Track layout and signalling arrangements around the Charing Cross loop when it opened in 1914. The facing crossover was removed as part of the work and a 'king' lever was installed to allow the signalling to operate automatically when required.

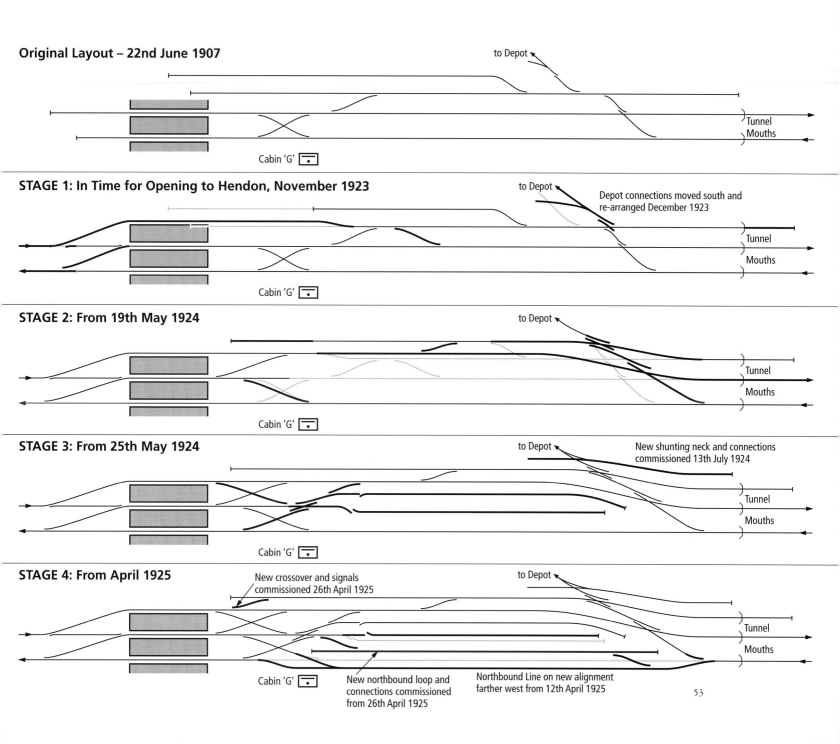

Original Layout – 22nd June 1907

to Depot

Tunnel
Mouths

Cabin 'G'

STAGE 1: In Time for Opening to Hendon, November 1923

to Depot

Depot connections moved south and
re-arranged December 1923

Tunnel

Mouths

Cabin 'G'

STAGE 2: From 19th May 1924

to Depot

Tunnel

Mouths

Cabin 'G'

STAGE 3: From 25th May 1924

to Depot

New shunting neck and connections
commissioned 13th July 1924

Tunnel

Mouths

Cabin 'G'

STAGE 4: From April 1925

New crossover and signals
commissioned 26th April 1925

to Depot

Tunnel

Mouths

Cabin 'G'

New northbound loop and
connections commissioned
from 26th April 1925

Northbound Line on new alignment
farther west from 12th April 1925

53

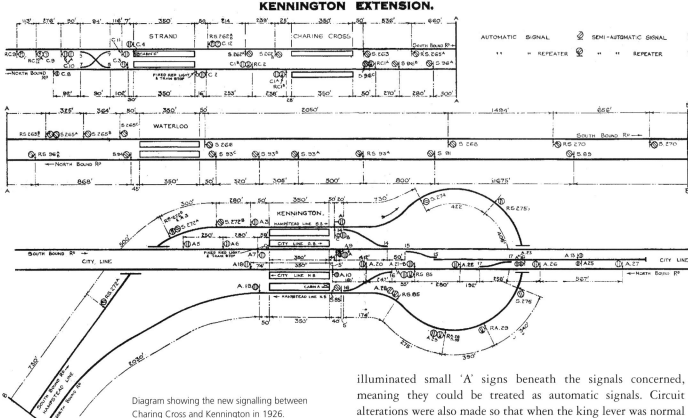

KENNINGTON EXTENSION.

Diagram showing the new signalling between Charing Cross and Kennington in 1926.

Following experience gained at Strand it became evident that where intermediate signal cabins were unmanned and working automatically, delays sometimes occurred; drivers had always to treat the signals as semi-automatic, meaning that in case of failure they were unable to pass them at danger. To address this, a programme began to install so-called 'king' levers, the first new installation being at Hampstead from 15th October 1922. When the king lever was pulled over in the frame it locked the running levers in position (which kept the routes safely locked) and illuminated small 'A' signs beneath the signals concerned, meaning they could be treated as automatic signals. Circuit alterations were also made so that when the king lever was normal (and the 'A' signs extinguished) any signal levers pulled over would only clear the signal for a single train, as elsewhere. By 1926 king levers were installed at Strand, Camden Town, Hampstead, Brent, Hendon Central and Colindale; the king lever at Camden Town just operated the through signals at Mornington Crescent.

One unusual signal on the extension was a semaphore mounted over the tunnel mouth at the north end of Hendon tunnel. This hand-operated device was nothing to do with train operations but was used as part of the eyesight testing regime—staff who had failed more conventional tests were permitted to demand a 'practical' test using this signal. It is still in situ but your author, though spending some years on the Northern Line, has never found anyone who remembers it being used.

PART FIVE
POWER SUPPLY AND RAILWAY OPERATIONS

Power generated at the Lots Road power house was transmitted at 11,000 volts via under-street ducts to Earls Court station, thence along the District Railway to Charing Cross substation. Since the Hampstead's connection with Charing Cross (District) wasn't built, it was necessary to construct a deep-level duct beneath Villiers Street which linked to the south end of the Hampstead's station at Charing Cross; the duct carried 11,000 volt feeders to the Hampstead's substations at Euston, Belsize Park, Golders Green and Kentish Town as well as local 600 volt feeders that served the south end of the line. Each substation had its complement of transformers and switchgear and a number of rotary converters that produced the 600 volts dc required for traction, lighting and lifts; usually two 800kW rotaries were provided, though Belsize Park had two 1200kW rotaries while at Charing Cross the Hampstead took its share from four 1500kW rotaries provided for the District and Bakerloo. Additional transformers produced dedicated signalling and lighting supplies, and supplies for the air compressors for the lifts and signalling equipment, also located at the substations. Each substation was permanently manned by an attendant who kept an eye on the rotaries and switched traction current on and off as necessary, including in an emergency if he received an urgent phone call requiring him to do so.

When the railway was extended to Edgware an additional substation was required at Burnt Oak; this was also equipped with rotary converters but the substation was arranged for automatic working, being remotely controlled from Golders Green. This was not only the first automatic substation on the Underground, but the Railway Engineer claimed it was the first automatic traction substation in the UK and the largest automatic electrical substation built so far. It was equipped with two 1200kW rotaries, with space for a third, and drew power from Lots Road. The takeover of the City & South London Railway in 1913 gave rise to an early decision to replace its unusual 5-wire direct current power supply system and install conventional high-voltage distribution

Cover and sample page of the Hampstead's first rule book.

to new substations. As part of this the Hampstead's substation at Euston was enlarged into part of the space occupied by the recently-closed Melton Street station building next door. At some date before 1923 a supply of electricity was obtained from the Metropolitan Railway which could be switched in an emergency onto the Hampstead Railway lift main from switches at Euston; if the Lots Road power supply failed the Met supply enabled all lifts that had stalled in the shafts to be moved to the top landing so the occupants could be released. When the Hampstead Line was extended from what became Strand to the Charing Cross (Embankment) station via the new loop, the existing cable tunnel was breached twice and the power lines were laid along the surface of the ground into Charing Cross substation via a temporary shaft at the north end of Embankment Gardens; the power cables were later re-laid in the new northbound tunnel, where they are today. The extension to Kennington in 1926 required a further substation south of Waterloo, built next to Lambeth North (Bakerloo) station and connected by a cable shaft to the Northern Line, below.

In 1931, to cope with enhanced train services, a new substation was opened at Hendon Central, also remotely controlled from Golders Green but this time using the new-fangled mercury arc rectifiers of the 'steel tank' type, another first for the Hampstead Line and an event which was so successful that for another thirty years or so all new rectifier equipment was mercury arc type. Unusually, Hendon substation normally drew an electricity supply from the Metropolitan Railway power station at Neasden via new ducts under the North Circular Road, suitable payments being made (the Underground and Metropolitan had various reciprocal agreements relating to power supply). In the 1920s and 30s some new substations opened to meet the increasing thirst for power. As part of the reconstruction of Leicester Square station, a new substation was opened there on 10th March 1935, remotely controlled from Charing Cross. A new substation was built at Edgware (opened in 1939) anticipating extension of the line to Elstree and the link to the old GNR line, to be electrified. This drew power from the North Metropolitan Power Supply Company at Wood Green, high voltage power coming via cables alongside the main line railway tracks from Alexandra Palace to Highgate and thence to Edgware; the substation was remotely controlled from the electrical control room at East Finchley, rather than Golders Green. Underground trains never made it west of Mill Hill East owing to the War, and subsequent railway closure required alternative arrangements to be made, the whole of the Golders Green-Edgware branch being arranged to draw its normal supply of current from the National Grid during the early 1960s.

In the 1950s the old rotary converters along the Hampstead Line were finally replaced by modern solid state equipment, and in the 1960s the mercury arcs followed. As part of this scheme a new substation opened at Camden Town in 1950, just north of the station building in Hampstead Road; initially this was controlled from Charing Cross, but by the late 1950s all substations north of Euston (inclusive) were arranged for automatic operation from East Finchley control room. The old substation at Charing Cross was inconveniently situated underground (alongside the District Line) and the entire affair was entirely replaced by a stylish new substation at surface level in 1957. With modern equipment all substations are today unmanned and controlled remotely from one single point.

At each substation site there was a gap in the conductor rails to separate electrically one section from the next. It was soon recognised that the possibility arose of a train stopping with one of its motor cars straddling the gap and bridging it electrically, enabling a dead section to be livened up with consequent danger to all concerned. To reduce the risk of this, a special indicator sign was placed just before each gap; drivers had preferably to stop at the sign if it were illuminated or if this were not possible they had to try and get the whole train beyond the gap to minimise the time it was bridged. These signs were fitted quite soon after opening, if they had not been there at the start. The original design of indicator is unknown, but from the early 1920s a new design appeared comprising a triangular pattern of red lights on a white triangular plate. The same pattern is still in use, together with a repeater for use where sighting is poor, where the lamps and plate are yellow. As originally equipped, current rail gaps were installed at the nearest point to the cable feeders, and as these often came down lift shafts the gaps were frequently located in the middle of platforms. This was soon identified as unnecessarily increasing the risk of pick up shoes straddling the gaps and during the early 1920s they were all moved, usually to a nearby position immediately beyond a platform so that a train finding itself off current could berth in a platform without bridging a gap.

It was also found that traction current sections were quite large so if there was trouble it was not always possible for trains to reach a convenient crossover (for example if the current was off at Camden Town it had to be discharged all the way to Euston, preventing trains from the south reaching Mornington Crescent crossover to reverse). There were some current rail gaps near crossovers but these were bridged by cables at special disconnection points that required tools to remove and were hardly conducive to their use. After the First World War a programme ground slowly into action to install (usually) four gaps at emergency reversing points bridged by easy-to-operate switches which could be pulled by qualified station staff; this enabled tracks on the OK side of the crossover to be charged with current while leaving the incident area dead. Many of these switches are still in use but for all sorts of reasons there is huge reluctance to use them except in the direst of circumstances.

Operation of the trains was attended by the prospect of using power unnecessarily and the engineers established that it was possible for trains to coast considerable distances without losing much time but saving quite a lot of energy. At first all the tunnel lights were left on permanently and where it was determined trains ought to begin coasting the normal lamps were replaced by distinctive blue lights. From 18th November 1907 it was decided to switch the tunnel lights off during the day (presumably further to save energy) and the coasting positions were then marked by painting a ring of tunnel segments white. From the 1920s characteristic white, diamond-shaped signs were installed in the tunnels instead, some still visible on the Northern Line. In the first thirty years of the Hampstead, coasting was considered very important and metering was even placed in train driving cabs to measure performance, with drivers being paid a coasting bonus if they achieved the required savings (the coasting bonus was stopped in 1923, though coasting was still measured for a few more years).

Short trains were apt to catch passengers on the hop, especially if anyone were waiting at one end of the platform and the train thundered to rest at the other. To avoid too much difficulty numbers were painted prominently along the walls just above the tilework (or occasionally on headwalls) denoting where the front of the corresponding length train should stop, the objective being to position whatever length train it was close to both entrance and exit. In the 1930s when train lengths had become less erratic neater stopping marks with a black number on nearly square white ground were fixed onto the track or tunnel side instead (where trains of any length should stop a diamond shape was used).

Emergency planning exercised tube managers even in the early days. The most worrying events involved arcing of traction current, or somebody on the line, where current had to be removed quickly. The tunnel telephone circuit was found wanting, especially if station staff were out of earshot of the bell, and from around 1917 a range of different arrangements were tried. The tunnel telephone circuits were reconnected straight through to the substations, but from the early 1920s the process was automated so that the mere action of clipping a telephone handset to the wires (or, indeed, even pinching the wires together) took the current off immediately, leaving the driver to explain the circumstances to the substation attendant, summoned by a distinctive alarm bell). Unfortunately the existing train telephones would not work on this system so the in-cab units were removed and drivers had to collect a handset at the start of each shift; these had to be carried around in a little wooden box, much to the inconvenience of all concerned and a relentless replacement bill (in recent times trains have had handsets fitted in the cabs again). So that station staff retained the facility to get current off quickly in an emergency new telephones in sealed boxes were installed on station headwalls; these were connected directly to the tunnel telephone circuits. In later years it was found these seldom-used instruments didn't always work because they became packed with dust that made the tiny contacts unreliable; robust push buttons were retro-fitted as an additional precaution—staff were now instructed to lift the handset and push the button to ensure satisfaction. As part of this programme the tunnel lights automatically switched on if current were removed. These changes resulted in the loss of direct station to station circuits which had then to be replaced by new ones between telephone switchboards at adjacent stations. Facilities were later augmented by additional telephone instruments at station headwalls to facilitate emergency 'station-to-station operation' during signal failures, the special instruments being connected into the circuit by plugs at the station switchboard.

Signal failures offered interesting challenges. The Underground's managers recognized that failure of just one signal could cause a succession of trains to get stuck in a tunnel, each with hundreds of passengers on board and with no convenient means of getting them out. The Board of Trade Railway Inspectorate reluctantly agreed that where automatic signalling was in force then under certain conditions trains could pass a signal at danger at extreme caution. This is not the place to examine the volatile experiences of the Bakerloo and Piccadilly but simply to say that on the Hampstead Railway a driver finding an automatic signal at danger had to wait one minute then despatch his

Examples of examination papers undertaken by staff qualifying for various grades in the 1920s.

conductor to walk forward along the tunnel with his lamp to see if he could ascertain why. If he discovered a train ahead then he had his answer; if he got to the signal ahead and found it clear then some kind of failure was implied if, on returning to his own train, the signal there were still at danger. Only then was the driver permitted to proceed (very cautiously) to the next station and report the matter—clearly this procedure could not avoid a lengthy delay. Station staff at stations either side of the suspected failure would then institute a system of 'cautioning' where trains would be authorized to proceed at caution between the affected stations ignoring intermediate signals. Staff used special forms and the station-to-station telephone to communicate with each other, a process which might be called 'telephone block' working but which is still familiar today as 'station-to-station' or 'point-to-point' working. Where drivers were required to pass a signal at danger they were instructed to isolate their tripcock to avoid uncontrolled emergency braking (but had then to stop normally to reset it and remove the isolation). Where a semi-automatic signal

was suspected to have failed a driver was forbidden to pass it at danger without the personal permission of the station master or signalman, the former being required to pilot each train over any points or crossings along the route. Points were at first equipped with electric track locks and mechanical locking bars and it was then considered quite unnecessary to secure them by hand.

Suffice to say that these rules continued to be refined over the next few years, mainly to speed up the process and close safety loopholes. The 1914 rule book allowed a driver at an automatic signal suspected of failure to proceed on his own initiative after one minute if he could see the line ahead were clear, but the conductor had to ride with him to help keep a look out. If the driver could not see a sufficient distance ahead then the luckless conductor had to walk in front of the moving train and stop it by red handlamp if he saw a train ahead or something else untoward (it is difficult to imagine a conductor pursued by a train doing so with much enthusiasm). In either case normal running was forbidden unless two consecutive signals were then passed at clear, as a short train ahead could leave a green light behind it for a couple of hundred feet. Having reported a genuine failure the station master could caution subsequent trains to apply the same procedure or, after discussing the matter with the divisional inspector, institute station-to-station working as before. In 1913 the mechanical locking bars and ground locks on points were removed (as unnecessary); thereafter, where semi-automatic signals failed, any points having to be traversed had to be secured by hand, much as today. A further refinement in the 1920s was to fit motor cars with 'control governors' that detected that there was sufficient air in the braking system to ensure a train would stop when the brakes were applied. This governor (a pressure operated switch) also detected the tripcock was active and disconnected the motoring circuit if there was insufficient air or the tripcock was isolated. Although a cut-out switch was provided in case the governor failed it was sealed to prevent misuse and it was not considered desirable to unseal it during a signal failure. Henceforth a driver passing a signal at danger had to drive the train slowly past and get tripped each time (still the position today), though if station-to-station working were put into operation the authorizing form allowed the driver to cut out the tripcock and unseal the bypass switch.

A great deal of knowledge was required of the staff, and trainmen were expected to avoid trouble where it was avoidable and to extricate themselves from it when trouble descended. Foremen motormen were a source of experience and advice but sound training at the outset was essential. From the very start a motormen's training school was established in the depot at Golders Green. Virtually a complete train's worth of equipment was installed and connected up, but the equipment was laid out so that its operation could be viewed and explained, together with huge diagrams showing how it worked. The weekly journal *The Electrician* thought this to be the first school of this type and possibly reflected experience being wanting on the other tube lines. The exact date of its demise is not known but from 1920 the Underground opened a central training school at Lambeth North, also plentifully supplied with real train equipment, and it is likely that the equipment from the Golders Green school was shifted there at the same time. Golders Green probably served for a while as a training school for most of the other tubes (though prior to 1920 the District also had their own motormen's school at West Brompton). Motormen were given comprehensive instruction about dealing with trouble during their journeys and were fully expected to identify all faults and even to sort out irregular operation of the live electrical contactors if necessary. Certain faults, or faults likely to occasion serious delay, were to be dealt with by simply calling on the following train to render assistance.

Serious incidents were also expected occasionally. Each train included at least one sealed sheet steel toolbox containing a substantial range of implements likely to be of help when catastrophe struck, including ever-useful items such as a hammer and ball of string. Optimistically, each individual tool box had its own unique set of three keys, the correct one requiring to be with the driver in charge of the train, with two complete spare sets of which one was in the charge of the line's Leading Motorman. Quite what the logistics were of ensuring the right driver had the right key(s) on the right train are quite unknown. If the trouble were more serious then ominous-sounding 'wreckage outfits' would be called for. These were kept in sealed cupboards located in each of the crossover tunnels and contained more serious equipment including crowbars, lamps, carpenter's tools and many other useful items including a whole range of hammers, no doubt used for all the more delicate adjustments.

In case of real trouble a breakdown gang was available 24 hours a day; this had access to a breakdown car filled with what were described as 'special appliances', timber etc, and doubtless more hammers. The car was to be summoned when it became evident the problem was beyond the capability of the wreckage outfit. The nature of the car, and whether a rail vehicle or road vehicle, is not stated but it was kept at Golders Green and a road vehicle is suspected simply because a serious calamity would make it difficult to get the car to site by rail. By the end of 1907 a whole organization had grown up around the need to deal with breakdowns efficiently. The home addresses of eighteen senior officials was made available to staff who had to advise them as necessary of any out of hours breakdowns on any of the three Yerkes tubes; eleven further breakdown staff were dedicated to

The control office for the three tubes at Leicester Square in 1911. The telephone exchange panels, barometer, headway and train interval clocks are highly visible; these special clocks could be connected to various points on each railway to monitor the service.

were not on the telephone isn't clear (one of the Hampstead's emergency men even lived as far away as Poplar). In addition, emergency men were dotted around the network to deal with routine problems, like telephone and signal linemen, and carriage examiners (or 'mechanical men'). By late 1907 all the emergency men across Yerkes's tubes had been pooled and redeployed to regular stations where they had ready access to the trains and equipment they looked after.

By 1926 the organization had become more sophisticated. The 'wreckage outfits' had long gone, to be replaced by less American-sounding 'breakdown tackle' which was now more conveniently located at the key stations Highgate, Hampstead, Golders Green and Strand. The London Fire Brigade had an arrangement which could deploy 'special emergency equipment' held at their headquarters in Southwark which included a petrol electric emergency tender with easily portable equipment on it, and a breakdown tender with heavy lifting gear that included jacks and a crane; there is no longer any mention of the tube lines having their own breakdown equipment. Various emergency staff were stationed at Colindale and Camden Town (mechanical), Edgware, Golders Green, Highgate and Camden Town (signals) and Golders Green (cables), with other emergency staff pooled with other lines, with (for example) permanent way emergency teams at Lillie Bridge and London Road. The locations of these people changed considerably over time. After London Transport was formed in 1933 breakdown arrangements were reinforced by instituting a network-wide breakdown organization under the rolling stock engineer. The Second World War caused further restructuring and at its conclusion breakdown engineers and breakdown foremen were permanently on call and three breakdown gangs were deployed around the network with dedicated emergency vehicles filled with useful heavy duty equipment (the fire brigade could still provide additional heavy equipment if required, but would not normally be called out). Fixed breakdown equipment was available at Edgware depot, Golders Green depot and Camden Town, amongst other places.

Having mentioned staff several times it should be said that staff institutes were provided from quite early days to provide both

fixing trouble on the Hampstead Line alone with three more staff providing network coverage for urgent specialist work, like carpentry. Few of these on-call people had immediate access to the public telephone system and the more senior officials had to be connected directly to the UERL's railway telephone network by expensive private wire. Quite how staff were advised when they sustenance and entertainment as required, but canteens, as such, did not arrive for several years. Staff had therefore to bring food with them if they wanted to eat, but were provided with time within their duties to do so. This was not entirely uncontroversial as it was found necessary to remind gatemen and conductors not to hang their meal baskets on the train line angle cocks between the cars or on the cable jumpers, the former looking like a convenient hook but capable of isolating the train's brakes. A staff institute was certainly provided at Golders Green by 1928, together with a mess-room that made hot food available at cost (mess-rooms serving food came later to be known as canteens). Canteens also appeared at Edgware, Hendon Central and Camden Town and all were also used by busmen. A staff institute had also opened at Camden Town prior to the Second World War.

The Hampstead Tube carried heavy traffic on bank holidays, especially at Hampstead and Golders Green which served those seeking the fresh air and holiday fairgrounds on Hampstead Heath. While this was a useful source of much-needed revenue it presented some formidable crowd control problems. Extra and longer trains were usually arranged, together with additional staff. Incredibly the arrangements for the first bank holiday on 5th August 1907 required no fewer than thirty police on duty at Golders Green to patrol the station entrances, with a further four constables and an inspector within the station; this was far beyond the railway's police resources so they were all supplied by the Metropolitan Police 'S' division, no doubt accompanied by a substantial bill. It is impossible to conceive what imagined criminality was anticipated by such vast law enforcement resources at this remote outpost. The railway staff was even candidly advised that if insurmountable difficulties arose within the station (beyond that which the entire station staff with five supporting police could handle) then the police inspector could draw in some of his resources from outside. A more modest contingent from 'S' division was also deployed in and outside Hampstead station, whilst 'Y' division provided a similar contingent at Highgate. 'Y' division also provided two constables to patrol the station at Camden Town under the station master's orders, and instructions pointed out darkly that 'a large number of constables' would patrol

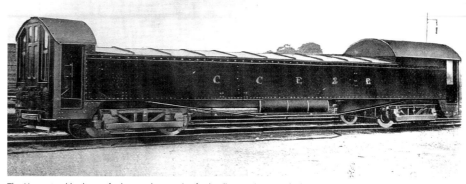

The Hampstead had use of a battery locomotive for hauling engineer's vehicles when current was discharged. The 80 batteries were slung along the lower portion of the body; there was an equipment compartment at one end. This locomotive (with a similar one on the Piccadilly) was built by Hurst Nelson in 1905 and was also used to equip the Hampstead and Piccadilly Lines.

outside the station. Suffice to say that the following August bank holiday the entire police presence was vastly scaled down, now being in the hands of the company's own meagre contribution of five constables and three ticket examiners supported by just four Metropolitan Police officers. Bank holidaying on Hampstead Heath remained popular for years and generated a great deal of publicity material, nevertheless numbers proportionately diminished over perhaps fifty years. By 1928 visitors getting there by Underground had fallen by about 20 per cent but was still sufficient to be an operating headache; Hampstead was one of several stations where inwards traffic was regulated by bells operated by platform staff signalling to staff and police at ticket hall level who were controlling incoming traffic.

Although the railway opened with a very efficient telephone system, some means of centrally controlling events quickly became a priority. At first the telephone operator at Leicester Square took responsibility for monitoring the movement of senior officials and repairmen but within two years a dedicated post was established to co-ordinate train services across the three tubes, partly replicating what had already happened on the District. A control office was set up Leicester Square and over time the controller acquired priority telephone circuits to key points and rudimentary means of monitoring the train service by plugging in special headway clocks and, later, service interval recording clocks to certain track circuits on each line. When the railway telephone network was automated in 1939 the controller acquired a suite of direct lines to key officials and the means of interrupting conversations on the automatic circuits. The controller's job was not intended to undertake the duties better done by local staff but to co-ordinate activity and make strategic decisions in support of local signalmen, for example to strengthen or reduce services if conditions required it, and to take an overview of how best to get the service on schedule after a lengthy incident. Perhaps inevitably the role grew to the point where each line had its own controller, the Hampstead and City & South London had its own controller from 1926.

The impact of introducing air-operated doors affected operations by reducing the numbers of train staff. As stated already the original, so-called 'gate stock' trains had a conductor (later styled guard, possibly from the 1913 rule book) at the front and rear with 'gatemen' at all the intermediate positions; thus a driver, front and rear guard and three gatemen would be required to operate the five pairs of platforms on a 6-car train. When air-operated doors appeared from 1923 the train's staff complement was reduced to a maximum of three, a driver and a leading and rear guard, each guard operating one portion of a train controlled from a position at the trailing end of each motor car (so only one guard was required on a short train with only one motor car). From 1928 it was felt that with adequate platform attendance in the rush hours a train could perfectly well be managed by a single guard at the rear of the train (at the leading end of the rear motor car) and train circuits were altered to make this possible. From that point a driver and guard remained the standard crew on what became the Northern Line until the introduction of the 1995 stock, and fittingly for this book the last crew-operated train on the entire Underground was a 1959 stock train that departed from Edgware on 27th January 2000.

PART SIX

CONNECTIONS AT GOLDERS GREEN

The UERL quickly had its eyes on the potential traffic that might be generated in the swathe of land between Golders Green, Hendon and Edgware and had supported the Edgware and Hampstead Railway in order to capture it. Since construction could not immediately be afforded, it was decided to develop the traffic by means of a dedicated bus service between Golders Green and Hendon (the Bell Inn) just over a mile away, not that there was a great deal in between. The UERL was not then in the bus business (that changed in 1912) so they arranged that the vehicles and drivers be provided by Messrs Birch Brothers of Kentish Town, the Hampstead Railway itself supplying the conductors who were under the authority of the Golders Green yardmaster; the cash they collected was paid in to the booking clerk there, who also kept the tickets when not in use. It was evidently felt that bus and train conducting skills were comparable and to encourage honesty the Hampstead's travelling ticket inspectors were empowered occasionally to travel on the buses to keep an eye on things; they probably welcomed the opportunity for a bit of fresh air (and the temptations of the Bell Inn). At first staff living in Hendon were charged the full fare if they used the bus, but from January 1908 a concession was grudgingly offered to staff in full uniform that they could travel free if there were space (though the conductor had to give permission in person and record the employee's badge number on his waybill).

The first agreement between the Hampstead Railway and Birch Brothers was dated 8th August 1907 and required a minimum of 24 buses each weekday (with an option as to Sundays) to begin retrospectively from 28th July and to operate for a minimum of a year, then from month to month until the agreement was terminated. The initial timetable required a more frequent service running at 12- or 24-minute intervals depending on time of day, journey time just ten minutes. Birch's were to deal with all costs (except conductor) while the Hampstead Railway was to fix the timetable and fares, manage the ticketing and retain the revenue, but pay Birch's a shilling a complete mile operated out of which they would meet their costs and profit. Motor buses supplied from a garage at North Finchley were used at first but were not sufficiently reliable and were replaced by horse-drawn vehicles from December when the agreement was adjusted. A later agreement of 25th February 1908 allowed an increase in charges to one shilling and fourpence a mile, and this was renewed on the same basis later in the year, to expire 1st December 1910 and with a ¹/₂d retrospective increase in charges for period until 30th December 1908 but reducing to 1s 3¹/₂d thenceforth. In 1909 the agreement was renewed until December 1911 and in July 1910 the agreement was subject to significant change. It appears the earlier service was by then being operated by three vehicles (there had at first been just two) and a fourth was now required that pushed the daily trips up. A new minimum of 66 a week were required and a sliding scale of mileage payment per trip agreed, ranging between 1s 6d for 132 trips or fewer and 1s 3¹/₂d for up to 238 trips.

The Hampstead was keen to integrate the bus and train services. From 13th September 1907 the railway ticket collectors were supposed to watch out for the appearance of the Hendon bus and ring a bell when they saw it hove into sight; the conductor of any train thinking of departing was, on hearing the bell, instructed to remain firmly at rest until anyone staggering off the bus had made it to platform level and boarded safely (it isn't obvious how the conductor would know this had happened). In the other direction train conductors had to be careful to let passengers retain tickets available on the bus instead of collecting them on the train. Although buses ran during the day, evening services at first stopped with an 8.35pm departure from Golders Green but from 1908 were extended until 11.59pm, presumably reflecting demand. Tickets issued on the bus were of the 'bell punch' type while tickets issued at stations were of a two-part type where the train portion could be detached by collecting staff on completion of the rail portion. When the four Golders Green non-stop trains were introduced in 1909 connecting 'non-stop' buses were arranged, doing the one-mile journey from Hendon in an exhilarating 12 minutes (noting the non-stop horse bus took longer than the stopping motor bus used at first). In October 1911

The forecourt at Golders Green with a horse bus to Hendon. The building on left is the cycle store, soon extended at the North End Road end, past the tree, accommodated for some years within the roof line before being removed. The station entrance is behind the bus. Having passed through the ticket hall, passengers were presented with a subway on the left which took them to the stairs to the middle departure platform. As with all other stations, one way flow was maintained and stairs from the flanking arrival platforms brought passengers down to another subway to the right of the booking hall. An empty stabled car can be seen above the embankment top left and the roof of the car sheds are visible in the background to the right of the tree.

the Birch service was reputed to have been 'run off the road' by the introduction of London General Omnibus Company (LGOC) motor service 13, which operated between London Bridge and Hendon (Bell) via Golders Green over much of the route still operated today; through tickets were issued from 1st September. The LER was quick to formulate an agreement with the LGOC to preserve the existing through booking between Golders Green and Hendon (Bell). They had agreed as long previously as 1909 to support allegedly unremunerative LGOC services between Childs Hill and North Finchley in order to encourage feeder traffic to the station. In 1912 the UERL purchased the vast LGOC and developed a more active policy of providing feeder buses to outer London stations to help develop traffic, the outcome being that Golders Green became an immensely important transport interchange with the small yard outside the main entrance much expanded. Even before the LGOC was taken over arrangements were made to connect with Sunday excursion services; by 1911 one such route, the 53 operated

The busy cycle store at Golders Green.

between Golders Green and North Finchley and by 1912 the 84 was running to St Albans, attracting valuable Sunday day out traffic.

The Finchley Road itself was the happy recipient of tram services provided by the Metropolitan Electric Tramways on behalf of the Middlesex County Council, who recognised the tremendous potential of Golders Green as an interchange. Services to and from North Finchley began in 1909 and in the other direction services reached Cricklewood the following year. Trams eventually reached Barnet while the number 60 ran via Willesden to Paddington, though this was not intended as competitive. The Metropolitan Electric Tramways also came under indirect UERL control in 1912, though the network was still owned by the County Council. When London Transport assumed control in 1933 they did not support tramway operation and replaced these services by popular new trolleybuses along broadly similar routes.

To improve connection with tram services running along the Finchley Road a new ticket office was opened on the eastern side of the railway from 18th December 1911. At the station end it was built into the side of the embankment at the northern end of the site, linking into the existing subway network; it was connected to the Finchley Road by a long timber covered footpath running alongside the depot approach road and had an imposing cream faience entrance. At the Finchley Road end was a small entrance building flanked with awnings. A succession of through bookings with bus and tram services along the Finchley Road gradually

emerged. Cyclists were catered for on some scale and at Golders Green covered cycling accommodation was available free to station users and, it would seem, very popular. The cycle store comprised sheds alongside the north-western edge of the forecourt but it later shifted itself to the new exit to the Finchley Road at the east side of the station, releasing the space for revenue-earning purposes such as a café for waiting bus passengers. In 1927 the original ticket hall at Golders Green was slightly enlarged and received a passimeter ticket office, though a modified wall office was retained for the healthy season ticket traffic, which included the road-rail tickets.

Following station reconstruction the western arrivals platform (Platform 1) had been retained for those alighting from northbound trains and the usual routine was for the guards to open the doors alongside Platform 1 so people could disembark, then open the doors alongside Platform 2 for northbound passengers to get in, doors being closed in the same order. In 1927 a new exit from the north end of the Platform 1 was built, with steps that snaked down the embankment to deposit passengers close to the Finchley Road—it was far quicker than the hike to the 1911 ticket hall and the long covered way and was also convenient for the small yard built in the 1930s alongside the Finchley Road in which trolleybuses could turn round. This exit was immensely popular and passengers wanting to use it were beside themselves if a northbound train were routed through the middle road from which they couldn't get to it; if this happened, many disgruntled passengers obliged to get out on Platform 3 would wait for another northbound train if one were in sight and then charge through it en masse while both sets of doors were open, using it as a kind of bridge. It was great sport for guards alert to this to shut the Platform 1 doors before opening the others!

Though a little out of period one might perhaps observe that the closure of Platform 1 and the demands of automatic ticket control have seen both these later exits closed during the 1980s and has left Golders Green with just a main ticket hall and a very peculiar subway system where in effect one subway serves the northbound platform and the other mainly the southbound, purely because of the odd way the station developed.

PART SEVEN
TICKETS

By the start of the twentieth century Britain's main line railways had evolved a complex system of ticketing and fare collection whereby many journey options were available across company boundaries and bookings were catered for by a huge number of different types of ticket, a comprehensive stock of which had to be kept at every station. Unusual issues were catered for by using blank stock tickets that had to be filled out on demand but even so prodigious station-specific stocks had to be kept, with all the accompanying accounting and security difficulties. The Metropolitan and District railways tended to follow this practice but with fewer through fares, which simplified matters only slightly.

When the tubes arrived they were each regarded as essentially stand-alone affairs with an unsophisticated requirement for different ticket types, more like a tram service. The first lines had flat fares with tickets (no more than receipts) issued at the booking office but immediately handed in at the start of the journey; returns (if they were issued at all) comprised a separate receipt kept until the start of the return Journey. By the time the Hampstead Railway opened it was accepted that flat fares were unfeasible so a system had to be put in place to recognise that the correct fare had been paid for the journey undertaken. Hampstead fares varied from 1d to 3d according to distance, but cheaper workmen's fares were available until just before 8am and different sets of tickets (singles and returns) were required for these. Matters had been further complicated by the discovery that passengers wanted to make through journeys between one underground line and another, and they resented rebooking en route (at Euston and Tottenham Court Road ticket offices had been erected in connecting subways, but they were short-lived). All this meant that every ticket office then required individual sets of tickets for all the most popular journeys, much increasing complexity.

The Piccadilly had used a colour coding system whereby a different colour (or combination of colour and overprinted design) was used for each destination station to help ticket collectors recognise correct tickets; the Hampstead Railway managers did not seem to think this necessary and at first all tickets were buff coloured. The Hampstead Railway also had season tickets from the very start, though the take-up in the early days was quite small (it is suggested they were not well advertised). Certainly tickets were on issue for one and three months, and seasons with dual availability were issued in high proportion; thus many seasons from the centre were jointly available to (from examples referred to) Belsize Park and Highgate, Belsize Park and Tufnell Park, Golders Green and Highgate, Chalk Farm and Kentish Town, or Hampstead and Highgate; nevertheless tickets to specific single northern termini are also known, and were probably cheaper. From opening the Hampstead had through bookings available to the Piccadilly, City & South London and London & North Western Railway local journeys via Euston. Through bookings were extended bit by bit, the Bakerloo by 9th August 1907, Central London by 1st September 1907 (allowing the subway ticket office to close), District by 19th June 1908 (by walking along Villiers Street or from western end stations via Piccadilly Line and Leicester Square), and Great Northern & City from 24th July 1908, via Euston and Old Street. Over time the range was expanded, though certain bookings were later reduced, such as those to the L&NWR.

The proliferation of through tickets across the various tubes (each with its own style) encouraged these railways to co-operate with each other and allocate each station on the network its own unique 'station number'; the originating and destination station number were shown prominently on the face of the tickets—the Hampstead's range of numbers was 49–66, running north, in geographical order, Highgate branch before Hampstead; the number 49 itself was apparently reserved for the unbuilt station under Charing Cross (District), and 65 for the unbuilt 'North End'. This system was certainly in widespread use by November 1907 but seems to have evolved from earlier practice on the Central London. It didn't have a long life as a standard pattern of tickets was introduced from summer 1909 where each line had a distinctive coloured card and all tickets carried the UNDERGROUND cameo logo with layouts standardized, though the various features didn't necessarily arrive at the same time. The Hampstead Line colour was a pale lilac, and remained this colour until London Transport days.

During the time of the First World War the ticket system was adjusted so that from any particular station all bookings at the same fare were accommodated on just one ticket (called a zone ticket); the stations to which available were shown on the front (and if necessary the back) of the tickets together with the fare prominently displayed. After the Second World War it was apparent that ticket collectors rarely referred to the daunting lists of stations but had got into the habit of recalling the fare paid and the station of origin and could spot incorrect tickets on that information alone. From 1952 ticket designs were simplified to show only the fare and station of origin, and this approach lasted until and beyond the era of electronic ticketing.

Season tickets in their original form had a short life. The small take-up and suspicion that they encouraged use without additional payment (these days regarded as the whole point) meant they were soon superseded by bulk sales of single journey tickets, known as strip tickets. These were widely available from 1st October 1908 and were usually sold at a small discount, for example a strip of six Highgate-Camden Town tickets, each face value 1 1/2d, were sold for 8d, a discount of 1d. Strip tickets were undated and were cancelled when each ticket was presented; dating of ordinary tickets ceased at the same time so those too could be bought in advance. Issues of local season tickets were discontinued from the same date and through seasons from 14th October (those already issued remained good until expiry). A single ticket could also be used for two children, or one dog (an interesting insight into the values of the day). Strips were not always popular and were open to various kinds of abuse, so seasons were accordingly re-introduced from 1st July 1911 and remained in existence until travelcards rendered them unnecessary in the 1980s; the 1d and 1 1/2d strips were discontinued from July 1914 though higher value strips were not finally abolished until 1st February 1916. (The Carnet type tickets introduced in the 1990s were similar in many ways to the short-lived strip tickets).

At first the new seasons were only available within the LER, but from October 1913 through rates were introduced to the other tube lines as well, extended to the whole of the UERL from 1st May 1914. On the Hampstead Line there were 15 local season ticket rates (rates applicable to the Hampstead Line alone), and 41 through rates to the other lines of the LER—the highest through (quarterly) rate was 50 shillings between Golders Green and Hammersmith. By 1916 it is evident that most seasons were for periods of one or three months, but a few 6-monthly and annual tickets were also sold (it has been suggested from UERL records that monthlies superseded 4-weekly tickets in February 1916). Seasons for six and twelve months were twice and four times the quarterly rate with no further discounts. Seasons were also available for children (under 15) and junior clerks (up to 18).

Booking office staff were evidently not trusted to handle these and for some years seasons could only be obtained on demand from one of the Underground's two season ticket offices, one at Mansion House and the other at Oxford Circus, with the suggestion they could be ordered and collected at stations with adequate notice; this regime was later partly relaxed, for example in 1924 some of the more popular quarterly tickets were sold on demand at stations. From 1st May 1923 a small number of through seasons were introduced which included feeder journeys via bus or tram to and from stations in the outer areas; for some reason they were only initially available from Warren Street, Tottenham Court Road or Charing Cross to or from nine assorted destinations by road. They were not the easiest things to procure: they could only be purchased at Golders Green station, the Underground's season ticket office at Oxford Circus or White's Library, Broadway, Finchley Church End. The range of road-rail tickets was subsequently extended and they lasted until the late 1970s.

Weekly tickets seem first to have been tried on the Bakerloo in March 1925, and differed from seasons in they had fixed Sunday-Saturday validity and were available on demand (seasons required much tedious form filling and record keeping). Apparently judged a success they had spread to the Highgate branch from 4th July and stations Edgware-Hampstead (except Burnt Oak) from 13th August, but they became pretty much universal within the next year or so. The apparent success of these seems to have caused a change of heart about the ability of staff to sell season tickets, and from 1st July 1928 the season ticket offices were closed and all seasons were available at stations on successful completion of the necessary forms. The issue of distinctive rail-bus or rail-tram weekly tickets via Golders Green began from 15th April 1928 from all stations Euston-Kennington to eight road destinations. To make it easier for ticket collectors to spot an out-of-date weekly ticket, from 10th January 1926 a large numeral was overprinted on the face of the ticket; any of the numbers 1 to 4 were used according to a schedule issued by head office. Although booking clerks were encouraged to retrieve old weeklies it didn't really take very long for fraudulent customers to collect a set of tickets numbered 1 to 4 by not handing them in, and by 1931 familiar 'random' two digit overprints (01-99) were used, coupled with periodic changing of ticket colour (until 1939 when purple was standardized for adult weekly tickets). For the law-abiding the fixed-week of the weekly meant that immense queues tended to build up on Monday mornings and in later years a concession was granted that providing the old ticket was surrendered they could be renewed after midday on Saturdays (and from the 1960s, from 4.30pm on Friday evenings).

Season tickets for children used adult-style ticket stocks suitably overprinted across the top left corner. From the mid 1930s children's seasons and weeklies used different coloured stocks that made them more distinctive. Seasons could be purchased for any period between a month and a year, the prices being based pro-rata on the nearest quarterly rate ticket, but for these 'odd periods' blank card unpriced stock had to be used and one would be very strongly encouraged to order in advance so the clerk had the time to undertake the necessary research and calculation.

To reduce costs at quiet stations, nine stations across the Underground had miniature ticket offices fitted in the lifts during the mid 1920s, the liftmen being required to issue and collect tickets from each lift as well as operate the vertical transport. The proper ticket offices were normally closed but sometimes one or two automatic machines in the ticket hall were available to help out. On the Hampstead Line the only station affected was Mornington Crescent where by 1928 a mini ticket office was fitted

into each lift, including ticket counter, ticket office window, dating press, till and removable ticket racks. These remained operational until electronic ticketing arrived in the 1980s. These 'pedestal' offices (as they were known) were not able to handle weekly or season ticket issues and passengers had to apply for such things either in advance or at the other end of their journey; those ordering in advance (imagine the lift operator's heart sinking) set in train a process where staff at Camden Town prepared the ticket and paperwork with ticket and cash being transferred between stations by messenger.

Tickets were examined and collected assiduously, though for a brief time in November 1907 instructions were issued (perhaps unwisely) that passengers known to ticket collectors to hold current seasons were to be passed unchallenged—the regulations were soon changed back requiring everyone to show or deliver up a valid ticket. Seasons had to be surrendered immediately on expiry and those that were not quickly returned were actively sought out in case they were still being used. Tickets for Golders Green were usually collected or examined on the train once it had left Hampstead, since each car had its own staff and traffic was light and it presumably saved staff at Golders Green; collected tickets had to be placed into special boxes on the platform at Golders Green (when the wooden platforms at this station were rebuilt in the 1990s a quantity of very old tickets was found and is now in the London Transport Museum). Though the arrangement was cancelled in 1917 it was soon resurrected and carried on for a while even after the Hendon extension opened.

Automation crept in slowly. Some stations quickly received penny-in-the-slot type 'pullbar' ticket machines but by the 1920s a range of electrical passenger-operated ticket issuing equipment was much in evidence, especially at the busier stations, and this allowed booking staff to focus on the more complicated ticket types. Automation within the booking offices began in the early 1920s for tickets at the most widely issued fares. An early device was the 'Automaticket' machine, first trialled at Leicester Square. This was essentially a variant of the devices used to issue cinema tickets. Up to six ticket types were available, each released directly to the passenger from slots in the change counter, several tickets emerging at once, if required. These slightly speeded things up but were not an unlimited success and were supplemented (and eventually replaced) by banks of 'Rolltic' machines which could date and issue one or more tickets quite quickly from pre-printed tickets on a roll. The biggest development, originating in the late 'twenties but coming into its own in the 'thirties, was the AEG 'rapid printer'. At the push of a button this could print, number, date and shoot out onto the ticket counter up to three tickets a second of up to 12 different types from huge blank rolls of card, and if demand varied during the day the printing units could be changed over to something more suitable in only a few seconds. They were joined from the late 'thirties by a smaller and cheaper 'mini-printer' with fewer units and lacking the conveyor system, so booking clerks had to trouble themselves to pick the ticket up and hand it to the passenger (but it was still better than picking tickets out of the rack and hand dating them). By the time electronic ticketing took over in the 1980s all former Hampstead Line stations except Mornington Crescent had at least one 'rapid' or 'mini', though card stock was needed as a backup and at many auxiliary windows.

Revenue from tickets arrived as cash, mainly low value coin. Local banking was unheard of and all the cash was reconciled and bagged up in the ticket offices and conveyed to the main bank in a travelling cash box (a kind of moving safe) that was carried on certain trains each day after the morning rush hour. When the Hampstead opened, the cash box was carried on the conductor's platform of the 9.37am departure from Golders Green transferring under signature from the supervision of the clerk-in-charge to the conductor. At Mornington Crescent it was shifted across to the northbound platform by the station supervisor and thence travelled via Highgate and back to Charing Cross, arriving at 10.27am. It was then put in the joint charge of a traffic audit clerk and a representative of Messrs Deacon's Bank, being conveyed to their branch in Cockspur Street, about 200 yards away, where the cash was remitted. The empty cash box was then despatched back to Golders Green. While the box was in transit to Charing Cross the chief clerk at each intermediate station met the train and dropped in his own takings. The unfortunate conductor had constantly to push the box from one side of the gangway to the other to keep it out of the passengers' way (and at Highgate had to haul it from one end of the train to the other). Correspondence (mainly from the ticket office) was similarly transmitted by travelling despatch cases carried to and fro to Leicester Square on certain trains before the morning peak, an arrangement continuing until the 1990s. Used tickets had to be shifted to the ticket sorting office too; at first it seems the Hampstead shared the Bakerloo's ticket sorting office at Baker Street and ticket sacks had to be got there (via changes at Leicester Square and Piccadilly Circus) to arrive by 8.30am, but from 25th January 1908 the office moved to the spacious Westminster Bridge Road station (now Lambeth North), the vacated space apparently being replaced by the offices of the three tubes' lift engineer, previously at King's Cross (Piccadilly). Another chore for the Hampstead's train staff to worry about was the conveyance of parcels for Messrs W.H. Smith's bookstalls which sprang up at many stations (some for a while on the platforms, much to the concern of the fire brigade). The UERL didn't like parcels at all, but tolerated their carriage before 6.30am in connection with the lucrative bookstall traffic, parcels even being allowed to occupy passenger seats next to the conductor's position.

Conclusion

When opened in 1907 the Hampstead Railway was the last word in tube railway design. Many of the stations have stood the test of time and are little changed today, though, sadly, none of the original tiling designs have survived at platform level. The lifts stand out as a particularly robust design, with some lasting 80 years, far longer than is expected than from modern equivalents. It is hoped that this contribution to the Northern Line's centenary events will have shed just a little more knowledge about the early days of the Hampstead Railway and the incredible contribution it has made to the well-being of London.

Group 1: Early style CCE&HR tickets

T1: 6.7.1907

T2: undated

T5: undated

T7: undated

T3: date unknown

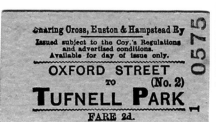

T4: date unknown

T6: 7.3.1908

Group 2: Later style tickets

T8: undated

T9: date unknown

T13: 7.9.1927

T14: style from late 1930s

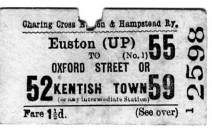

T10: date unknown

T11: 6.9.1931

T12: date unknown

Group 3: Through tickets

T15: 11.9.1907

T16: 11.9.1907

T17: 7.3.1908

T18: 25.6.1907

T19: date unknown

T20: 11.9.1907

T21: 13.9.1907

Group 4: Inter-modal tickets

T22: undated

T23: undated

T24: undated

T25: undated

T26: 1923